Inner Dialogue
with
Sai Baba

Geesje Lunshof

B.R. Publishing Corporation
[A Division of BRPC (India) Ltd.]
Delhi-110035

Distributed by:
BRPC (India) Ltd.
4222/1, Ansari Road, Darya Ganj,
New Delhi-110002
Phone: 3259196, 3259648
E-Mail: *brpcltd@del2.vsnl.net.in*

Geesje Lunshof
Houtrustlaan 16
2566 ZT The Hague
The Netherlands
tel/fax: 00 31 70 3648117

ISBN 81–7646–092–3

Published by:
B.R. Publishing Corporation
[A Division of BRPC (India) Ltd.]
3779, Ist Floor, Kanhaiya Nagar
Tri Nagar, Delhi-110 035
Phone: 7152140
E-Mail: *brpcltd@del2.vsnl.net.in*

Any royalty which may arise from the sale of this book will be donated to charitable Sai Baba funds throughout the world.

Cover-design: Jyothi Catell Sparks / Kees Denie
Lay-out: Marjo de Jong

Printed by:
BDH Printer
Delhi-110085

PRINTED IN INDIA

TO BHAGWAN SRI SATHYA SAI BABA

WHO IS SAI BABA?

Sri Sathya Sai Baba is the Avatar of this age. Avatar means the embodiment of God in a human form. As a world teacher He has come again to guide man in these critical times and to set the world right. He says, *"I have come to illumine the human heart with the light Divine and to rid man of the delusion that drags him away from the path of Inner Peace".*

Sai Baba has two ashrams in the southern part of India, in Puttaparthi and in Whitefield, where every year hundreds of thousands of people from all over the world gather to experience his love and to receive his blessings.

Sai Baba has not come to earth to start a new religion or cult. On the contrary, he emphasises the unity of all religions. He says, *"I have come to tell you of this Universal unitary faith, this Inner Self Principle, this Path of Love. All religions teach one basic discipline; the removal from the mind of the blemish of egoism, of running after little joys. Every religion teaches man to fill his being with the Glory of God, and evict the pettiness of conceit. Be convinced that all hearts are inhabited by the One and only God; that all faiths glorify the One and Only God. His adoration is best done by means of Love. Cultivate that attitude of Oneness between men of all creeds and all countries. That is the Message of Love I bring".*

As a teacher he guides the spiritual development of those who turn to him, at this moment more than one hundred million people, world-wide, and he is the great Motivator, both inner and outer. In India he has founded many schools and five universities where education is completely free. He has also built a number of hospitals, where everyone is given free medical care. In Puttaparthi one can find one of the most modern hospitals in the world in the field of heart and kidney transplantation and here too any treatment is totally free of charge.

The name Sathya Sai Baba is significant. Sai means Divine Mother and Baba means Father. Sathya means Truth. His mission is to bring back Truth in the heart of Man, so that Righteousness can be restored on earth.

"There is only one religion, the religion of love.
There is only one caste, the caste of humanity.
There is only one language, the language of the heart.
There is only one God and He is omnipresent".

- **Sathya Sai Baba**

ACKNOWLEDGEMENTS

I would like to thank Arjaan ten Hoorn, who was always ready to listen to a new "lesson" and who, more than even myself, was and remained convinced that it really was Sai Baba who made me write down these lessons. The certitude with which she stood behind me was an enormous stimulus for me to keep opening myself to the messages.

I also would like to thank Adinda van Schagen for taking on the Dutch proofreading as well as Ruth Willems, who took a great deal of time and energy in proofreading this English translation. Both have assisted me very lovingly by word and deed.

And then, Henk Meijer: thanks for the more than generous support I received from you almost immediately after you had read volume 1.

I also owe gratitude to Lucy Hofman for her dedication in planning a cover-design. In this respect I also would like to thank Kees Denie, Jyothi Catell Sparks and Marjo de Jong. Through their joint efforts the cover has come about.

To Marjo de Jong I owe extra thanks for the work she did in preparing the book for print. Thanks are also due to Larry Ajola, who took upon himself the final editing of the English manuscript.

Above all I would like to express my deep gratitude to Sri Sathya Sai Baba, for He is the one who gave me these lessons. Without Him, this book would not exist; I would not exist; none of us would exist. With a heart filled with gratitude, I ask You to teach me, each day anew, to open myself to Your Wisdom, Love and Divine Power.

Geesje Lunshof

TABLE OF CONTENTS

PART 2 : God Is One

FOREWORD

I have been given the honour to write some words as an introduction to the book you are about to read.

Right from the start you will be confronted with the doubts that Geesje Lunshof was seized with when she received these Lessons from Sai Baba. I am glad that in this respect she really made it difficult for herself, or else this work could not have come about as purely as it has. Fortunately Baba kept the awareness alive in her that writing down the material and distributing it was her duty, with the fortunate outcome that many may become acquainted with it and may benefit from it spiritually.

In the bibliography of Sai books there are some books based on messages of Sai Baba that come across to me as being totally in the spirit of Baba. These are the books written by Lucas Rally, Charles Penn and Little Heart, whose works have a place of honour on many a book-shelf of Sai devotees. In my opinion the book before us belongs in the same category, owing to the purity of intent, the selfless attitude and the profound light that Swami throws on His teachings. The book "Invitation to Glory" by Howard Murphet was my first introduction to Baba. I still remember, as if it were yesterday, that from the first page I knew that I had struck gold. On reading the first pages of this book I received again the same feeling that it is real, true and pure and most valuable for our spiritual walk through this life. In fact it is not just a book - it is a series of LESSONS to be studied repeatedly, with close attention, which offer new insights, discernments and perspectives into Baba's teachings and which will then reverberate in our daily life, for the good of ourselves and everyone and everything around us.

You know when our beloved Swami gives a discourse He always has some speakers-students, teachers or any other prominent devotees-speak before He does. We then listen very obediently to the "first course" but can't wait to hear the "main course", Swami Himself speaking, for that is what we came for! Well, start in the same manner with your reading, studying and ruminating upon the splendid material that is waiting for you. It is as a rich meal with many nutritious, spiritual dishes. Enjoy it and may Swami bless you abundantly while doing so. To Him the sole honour! Om Sai Ram.

Henk Meijer
April 1997, Whitefield (India)

FOREWORD

INTRODUCTION

This volume contains a collection of spiritual teachings, which have come to me from Sai Baba since August 11, 1991. Sometimes the messages I get are strictly personal, but usually they are of a general nature. The more personal teachings have not been recorded here, only those teachings which could also be significant to others. The process takes place in writing, by means of question and answer. A message often begins with a question, usually of a spiritual nature, which keeps on posing itself to me. The moment I write down such a question, the answer comes automatically to my mind, after which question and answer succeed each other until there is nothing left to ask any longer.

As said, the immediate cause of such dialogue can be a spiritual question, but it can also be a dream, in which Baba is present and which I do not completely understand, or a spiritual experience undergone by me, the meaning of which I can't quite grasp.

It took a long time before I had enough confidence to acknowledge that it really is Sai Baba who communicates with me in this manner. So, for the past few years I have only read these teachings to two friends and for the rest I did not have any idea what to do with them. In spite of my friends' assurance that it really could be no other than Baba, I was not so sure myself. "Just suppose that it isn't Him, that I myself am doing it, wouldn't that be terrible," I would think. "Then I really would have landed in an enormous ego-trap".

Slowly but surely I began seeing things in a slightly different perspective, for even if it was me, it was still a very pure and deep part of myself, to which I had no access whatsoever in normal daily consciousness. The answers were often so wise and so different from what I was able to conceive with my normal intelligence, that they could come from no other than my deepest soul, the Atma. And isn't that precisely what Sai Baba is, the deepest soul, the Atma, who resides in our hearts? This put me at ease in so far that it made me less diffident about asking spiritual questions. But still, I lacked the confidence to do more with the dialogues than reading them to one or two special friends. Of course to me they were of great value, especially the personal ones. Still I realised that a great number of the teachings could be of general interest. "Why worry," I would think then, "If Baba wants others to know of them, it will surely happen".

I continued with them; it had almost become second nature, that's how wonderful it was to communicate with Him in this manner and I often felt Him very close at those moments. But the feeling "what if it isn't Him, but me," kept gnawing at me and often even stopped me from taking up my pen to let Him work through me.

Until on 20 May 1993, on Ascension Day, a very special incident took place. Doctor Gadhia was in Holland, where he was to give a number of discourses. Doctor Gadhia is a very special devotee of Sai Baba, who had been raised from death by Him. Since that time, quite a few years ago, he materialises, on the orders and in name of Sai Baba, vibuthi (Baba's holy ash), with which he cures people. That day I had been invited for lunch at the house of Mona Jairam. Doctor Gadhia would be present and Mona had invited about twenty people. The idea was that doctor Gadhia would treat personal problems and reply to questions from those present. Miraculous things happened.

I was one of the last persons to enter the Puja-room (a small room in Mona's house arranged as an altar).

At first I only wanted to ask Doctor Gadhia for Baba's blessing, but in the small hallway towards the room I suddenly knew for sure, "Now I am going to ask if it is Baba, or if it is me, who answers my questions". I kept it neutral. "Doctor Gadhia," I said. "For some years I have been given written responses by Sai Baba to questions I write down. I am not sure though if it is really Sai Baba, who gives the answers, or if I am giving them myself. Could you tell me?"

He looked at me piercingly and said, "It is Baba". He asked me to take off my ring, place it in the palm of my right hand and close my other hand over it. He put his own hands over my closed hands and said a few Sanskrit mantras for me to repeat. After which he asked me to repeat the phrases, "Please Baba"... "Bless the knowledge"... "You give to me"... "For the people".

I couldn't believe my ears. "Please Baba, bless the KNOWLEDGE, You give to me for the people!" That was what he made me repeat! That was not how I had explained it to Doctor Gadhia. All I had asked was if it was really Baba with whom I communicated, and now I was made to understand that it was KNOWLEDGE, meant for the people!

"Open your hands now," he said. "Baba has blessed it". I opened my hands and in the palm of my right hand, around and underneath my ring, was quite an amount of vibuthi.

"Eat it," he said. "Through the ring Baba will give you inspiration". I couldn't believe my eyes or my ears. So, it was really true, and more than that, it was KNOWLEDGE, and I was allowed to give it to the people!

From that moment my confidence became greater. I dared, even though still in a limited way, to tell more people about it, and I dared to turn more often to Baba with my pen.

Another incident, some months later, took away any diffidence I still had left. This took place in India, at Sai Baba's ashram in Whitefield near Bangalore. I had been there for some days, when on 27 July 1993, after Darshan (the moment when Sai Baba walks past His devotees and pours out His blessings on them), I was introduced to Mr. Nanaiah. Mr. Nanaiah is the leader of Sriramanahalli, a cluster of villages in the surroundings of Bangalore, established for the poorest of the poor by People's Trust India, and for a couple of years supported by People's Trust Netherlands. People's Trust is a very special charity-organisation, entirely inspired by and based on the teachings of Sai Baba. Much to my pleasure, I was for some years the translator of the newsetter of People's Trust Netherlands, which was published twice a year. That was the reason that Harry van der Heijden, secretary of People's Trust Netherlands, introduced me to Mr. Nanaiah. "She is the translator of our newsletter," he said. "She does a good job for she is an English teacher". Mr. Nanaiah looked at me. "Now she is still an English teacher," he said. "But soon she will be a spiritual teacher". He said many more things, but all the time he came back to the fact that I would be a spiritual teacher. "You must hurry," he also said. "People are waiting for it". "How do you know all this?", I asked, stupefied. "I know," he said, smiling kindly.

"I sometimes communicate with Baba, He gives me spiritual lessons; is that what you mean?", I asked.

"Yes, continue with it," he said.

"But what should I do with them?" "Sai Baba knows. He is the Lord. Trust Him. He will lead you; leave it to Him".

For me this was one more confirmation that it really was and is Sai Baba, who writes through me. The incident took place unexpectedly and unasked for. There is no denying it.

Since that time, from the moment I returned to Holland, the teachings have been much more extensive and much more frequent. I think that this is due to the fact that I am now, more than previously, able to open myself up to them. He, Sai Baba, leads me in every field. I clearly notice this in my personal life as well. The more trusting I am and the more I am able to open up, the more often and the more clearly He gives his messages. "The answers are there, the questions are what it is all about," Baba let me know in one of the more personal messages. THE QUESTIONS ARE WHAT IT IS ALL ABOUT. Sometimes they are there, but very often there are no questions, there is only a state of BEING, of surrender to Him. A state of complete trust that He is there to lead us all, to be with us, mapping out a road for all of us, which we only have to follow; not doing anything ourselves, simply letting ourselves move along with the stream. The stream which could be a stream of love if only we would be willing to look at it that way. But before we can do so, a lot of garbage has first to be cleared away. Garbage in the form of memories, thinking patterns, happenings, impurities, doubts. So that, slowly but surely, we will very gradually move closer and closer to Him. Or put differently, He will move closer and closer to us.

In the summer of 1994 I was again for some weeks in Sai Baba's ashram in Whitefield. There I became filled with an intense feeling of gratitude, when on July 30 Baba was so gracious as to bless the first 23 chapters of the manuscript of this book during Darshan by laying His hand on it. To me this was the ultimate proof that the lessons really came from Him. At that moment I realised that, had Sai Baba not done this, putting this book on the market would, of course, have been out of the question, in spite of all above-mentioned considerations. I realized that there still had been deeply hidden feelings of doubt. "So, it is really Him," went through my mind and, "I am truly allowed to to share His messages with others".

Although Baba had already promised in 1994, a few days after His blessing, that he would sign the manuscript - He had come towards me, while I was holding the manuscript and a pen up to Him, and said very clearly, "I will sign, I will sign" and a few moments later, "not now, wait!" - this had not yet happened, even though I had been back to Him three times afterwards. I was prepared, kept the ever-growing manuscript at hand during Darshan, but I wasn't overly occupied with it. For Baba has His own time, and now it was up to Him. He would know when the time would be right to sign. It only remained for me to have confidence, to wait and see and to continue communicating with Sai Baba through my writing.

At the end of November 1997 I was scheduled to go to Sai Baba once again. The manuscript was now completely finished, the Dutch version as well as the English translation. Both manuscripts had been corrected several times and the Dutch version would go to the printer's immediately after my return from India. I intended to take only the Dutch manuscript, which I had given the same cover as intended for the book, showing the Sarva-Dharma symbol, symbol of the unity of all religions. Now that the book was completed, I hoped that Sai Baba would place His signature, as He had promised to do.

A few days before my departure for India I had a dream. In this dream I am in Sai Baba's ashram and at a certain moment Sai Baba walks towards me; He takes the **two** manuscripts that I have brought along and signs both of them. Well, that was clear; not only was I to take the Dutch manuscript, but also the English translation. And... Baba would sign this time, both manuscripts, no less.

As so often happens with things related to Sai Baba, it all turned out quite differently. Even though, once in the ashram - this time in Puttaparthi, His main ashram - I got good places during Darshan and Baba looked twice very clearly at the manuscripts, He didn't seem to have the intention to sign them. What to do? "Go to the public relations office and tell them you wrote a book, they usually give you a special place then," someone suggested. I did as told and the next afternoon I was indeed given a perfect place on the first row. Behind me were two women, a Dutch woman and an American, who asked me if I would let them look through the manuscripts I had laid beside me. They spent the time that was left before Baba came out, in reading jointly some of the chapters, one in English, the other in Dutch.

Marjo de Jong, the Dutch woman, told me later that the book had appealed to her right away. It answered several of her questions. She impressed upon me to prepare the publication of the book carefully. It was best not to do anything before I had contacted a friend of hers in the Netherlands, who most certainly would help me in carrying out the practical details. "As this is an important spiritual book," she said, "it should have a perfect appearance and I am most willing to help you with it". Once back in Holland, Marjo has indeed been of great assistance to me.

Jyothi Catell Sparks, the American woman, said that on seeing the cover, she had felt a shock of recognition. "This is the book I dreamt about," she said. About a year previously she had had a dream in which she looked at a book with practically the same cover as that of the manuscript she now had before her. Notably the Sarva-Dharma symbol was identical. In her dream she had flipped through the pages and found a photograph of the portrait of Sai Baba that she had just started! "Your book is the book of my dream," she said stunned. And she added, "I think this means that a photograph of my painting will be included in your book". The moment she said this, I knew, with an inner certainty, that this was indeed to be so; even though at that moment I knew nothing about her, or about the painting of which she spoke.

She told me that she was a portrait painter and that she had painted two portraits of Sai Baba. About a year ago she had started on the second painting, a life-size portrait of Sai Baba. She had brought this to the ashram a few weeks ago to offer it to Sai Baba as a birthday present for His seventy second birthday. When she came to Sai Baba's secretary with the canvas painting rolled up under her arm, he told her that she should have the painting framed and then go to the committee next door, which consisted of some six members, for initial approval. This committee would either accept or reject the gift. If it met with their approval it would be taken to Sai Baba. Two days later, when Jyothi had finished framing the painting, she took it to the committee. They accepted it and told her they would present it to Sai Baba. "But," she was told, "It was very likely that she would get it back the next day". "Because that's what usually happens with gifts for Sai Baba," it was explained. "Baba looks at the gifts, blesses them and then most of them are returned the following day". She was to come back the next day to find out how Sai Baba had reacted.

When she returned the next day, one of the committee officials came towards her with a big smile on his face. Not only was Sai Baba most pleased with the painting and wanted to keep it, He had also said that it must be placed in the Temple!

While telling me this, Jyothi was leafing through the manuscript and came across a picture of Sai Baba which I had added just before leaving. "There should be at least one photograph of Sai Baba in the book," I had thought. Again a shock went through her, this was the very photograph she had used for her first painting of Sai Baba. I was equally amazed at this particular "coincidence". Thousands of pictures have been made of Sai Baba and precisely the one I had chosen for the book, was the one Jyothi had used for her first painting of Him.

When Sai Baba came out, He walked closely past us on his way to the Temple as well as on his way back. Both times He looked in one glance at the three of us alternately, moving His right hand in a downward gesture as if wanting to say, "Take it calmly, it all fits in the great scheme of things".

All this made it clear to me why Baba had given me a dream just before leaving. Wasn't it because of this dream that I had not only taken the Dutch manuscript, but also the English one, without which no contact would have come about between Jyothi and me? But, in the dream Baba had also signed the manuscripts. Consequently, until the last day of my stay, I felt confident that this was going to happen and I always took both manuscripts with me to Darshan. The last day I got a front row seat. Was this the moment? When Baba walked past, I gathered up all the courage I had and asked, "Baba, an interview please for the book". He looked at me and said softly, "Wait, wait," and again He made the same downward gesture with His right hand.

Although now the chance had gone that He would sign, I was contented; more than that, I was filled with great joy. The "wait, wait" seemed to imply "I know all about it, it is good the way it is, just take it slowly". And why shouldn't I? For isn't Baba's time the best time?

However, once back in Holland, a feeling of doubt came over me. Suddenly I didn't understand anything anymore. The book was all set for the printer's and I would not go back to Sai Baba with the manuscripts anymore. Why then hadn't He signed them? Hadn't He said so three and a half years ago? And hadn't He, as an extra confirmation, given me a dream right before I left in which He signed the manuscripts? Not the galley-proofs or a book, no, very clearly two manuscripts! How could that be? Wasn't the book meant to go to the printer's after all?

While I was having these doubts, I came "by coincidence" across the same quotation of Sai Baba, on two consecutive days, in two different books which I had brought back from India. *"Which dreams are real? Dreams relating to God are real. If the Lord or your Guru appears in a dream, it must be the result of His Will, not due to any of the other reasons which cause dreams. It can never happen as a result of your wish"*. Only when I came again across the quotation in the second book, did it hit me. Of course, that was it! Sai Baba did sign the manuscripts! For, when He appears in a dream, it is reality! So, that was the solution to my problem. Baba really signed the manuscripts and in doing so He has given His consent. That this didn't happen physically,

8

surely was of no importance. I understood that this was a test, a test of my trust. For how could I claim to have an inner dialogue with Sai Baba, a dialogue which is often preceded by a dream or meditation, and then not acknowledge this dream to be true? Baba has indeed kept His promise. By doing so in a dream and not in our so-called reality, He has shown me, the way He also does in the teachings, that the dividing line between the inner and the outer Sai has merely been created by us, but does not really exist.

Sai Baba, in humbleness I dedicate this book to You and I ask You to kindly keep guiding me in everything I do.

"If you want to overcome body consciousness then attachment and hatred must go. Once the attachment and hatred go, duality will be destroyed. When duality disappears, ignorance will vanish. Therefore, the Vedanta has declared that it is only through wisdom that you can destroy ignorance and reach the ultimate. What is this wisdom that you should develop? Can it be gained by acquiring secular knowledge in the world? No. It does not deal with external phenomena at all; it deals only with internal experience. It is only when you have developed self-confidence that you will be able to develop a strong confidence in the Lord. If you do not believe in yourself, you cannot truly believe in God. When you have faith in yourself then you can have faith in God. To develop such a firm belief in yourself, you need to constantly engage in the practice of self-inquiry".

- Sathya Sai Baba

PART 1
Spiritual Teachings

The Portrait of Sai Baba as painted by Jyothi Catell Sparks

1
SLEEP

Question: Baba, are we closer to You when we are asleep?

Baba: No, you are closer to me when you are awake.

Q: Where are we when we are asleep? (During the dreamless sleep, I mean)

B: Nowhere. The body is resting at that moment, and your spirit has merged in the "All", in me.

Q: Is that a good condition?

B: It is a necessary condition, once in a while, but not ideal.

Q: Why not?

B: Because it didn't happen consciously.

Q: And when we die?

B: The aim is that your spirit merges consciously in me.

Q: And if that does not happen, if the same thing happens as during that non-ideal condition of sleeping?

B: Then you will come back again on earth to learn once again to be conscious in death.

Q: Is that the reason that I (and many others) often do not sleep well?

B: Yes.

Q: How can I learn to sleep well and still be conscious?

B: You cannot learn that. I can teach you not to attach too much importance to sleeping. Sleeping is not an exercise in dying, do not worry about that. Meditation is the exercise for this, concentrating on me.

Q: Still, there are also nights that I sleep very well, how can that be?

B: Sleeping is not ideal, but it is necessary. If your body needs it, I will make you sleep. If I see that your body is able to cope without sleep, I keep you in that condition

Q: But then my spirit merges in You unconsciously?

B: Yes, that is something which we must accept. It is not insurmountable, because you are born into your body each morning anew.

Q: But what about dreams, then?

B: Dreams are an intermediate stage. Your spirit passes through different stages of consciousness in order to finally reach the point where there is no consciousness anymore, or to wake up.

Q: But don't we need dreams?

B: That is precisely the reason that people need sleep. Besides, that condition of being without any consciousness is also necessary for your spirit. Your spirit needs being merged into the "All". The only less ideal fact is that this occurs unconsciously.

Q: And dreams in which You appear, Baba?

B: They are reality. Then I place myself in your consciousness to teach you something or just to be with you.

Q: Why does that happen during sleep?

B: Because you are then most receptive to me. You do not place anything between you and me. You accept what is happening to you. It is a gradual process. Your body has to get used to having me with you, to seeing me and talking to me. During sleep this happens very gradually.

Q: Am I in a special level of consciousness at such a moment?

B: Your spirit is with me then, or rather I am one with your spirit.

Q: Why are those dreams often so difficult to understand?

B: They are not difficult. You will understand the symbols I use when the right time has come. Symbols are the best method of communication because their truth penetrates into the center of your soul. What cannot be communicated in words can be communicated in symbols.

14

Q: Baba, why do You sometimes appear in my dreams, but most of the time You don't?

B: I come when you need a message from me. And also when you sincerely ask for it.

2
ANIMALS

15 September 1991

Question: Baba, You want us to live without violence, but we have learned it by watching the animals. Every-thing eats each other, so, why shouldn't man get the idea that eating meat is allowed?

Baba: In the animal world all are sacrifices for one another. But for whom should man sacrifice himself? For no one! His body does not serve to be consumed as food for other species. That is why he himself should not feed on other species.

Q: Yes, but what about lions and tigers? They are also not eaten by other species, so then, should they also not be allowed to kill?

B: Lions and tigers belong to the highest form of predators. Somewhere the link of eating and being eaten must stop, or else it would continue unendingly. Man would eat these predators and would, in turn, be eaten himself. With the predators, the process of continuously being eaten stops. That is one more reason why man should not lend himself to take part in the animal process of eating and being eaten. If even large mammals, like the elephant, do not take part in it, should man degrade himself to being a bloodthirsty animal? With man, a new evolutionary process begins in which the weaker is no longer threatened by the stronger. Unfortunately, many people are still trapped in their animal nature because of the countless lives they lived as animals. This must first be conquered, then man can go on and develop himself spiritually.

3
EVERYTHING HAS A SOUL

14 October 1991

I found two small buttons which I wanted to throw away.

Baba: Stop! Everything has a soul, also those two buttons. They are still alright. Don't throw them away.

Question: Yes, but Baba, who puts the soul in lifeless matter, is that You?

Baba: No, it is the user. Or, if it is not a question of mass production, but of artistic work, the one who makes them.

4
PEACE OF MIND

14 October 1991

During my meditation I heard Sai Baba say, "When you have peace of mind, there is a way out".

Question: Baba, what do You mean by "a way out"?

Baba: "A way out" is a way to escape the circle of reincarnation. Peace of mind is the only way to reach this. Peace of mind is a condition for immortality. Peace of mind is a condition in which you accept everything with equanimity.

Q: How do I reach peace of mind?

B: By doing your Sadhana (spiritual exercises).

Q: Do you mean meditation?

B: Among other things. I give peace of mind. I judge how far you have progressed with your peace of mind. You cannot judge that yourself. It is a question of inner peace at all times, even when things do not seem to go well. Acceptance is the key-word. Start with acceptance, then inner peace comes by itself.

Q: But can't I influence things?

B: Yes, but this must come from a calm heart, not from agitation. Be convinced of this: "I direct everything. Your life is in my hands, whatever happens. I have willed it so". Have faith in me! In my omniscience and in my compassion. I will never leave you. Nothing can go wrong. Accept this as the only reality, then you have peace of mind.

Q: Baba, this warm feeling in my heart, is that peace of mind?

B: No, that is bliss, my Ananda.

Q: Why is it not always there?

B: It is always there, but man himself hides it.

Q: How?

B: Ananda is a condition of BEING. The daily routine is a process of BECOMING. BECOMING conceals BEING, but BEING is always there. When BECOMING is experienced as BEING, you feel Ananda.

Q: So, if during my daily pursuits I am still able to experience BEING, that is when I experience bliss?

B: Yes, then you see, as it were, beyond the things that have to do with time.

Q: At such a moment I think that You are with me.

B: That is true, but I am always with you, not only when you experience it. Know that I am always there and you will always experience Ananda.

Q: But sometimes I think of You, during my work for instance, but I don't feel your Ananda.

B: Then you are too much involved in the process of BECOMING and you forget the process towards the state of BEING. It is not always possible here on earth. Your work implies BECOMING, because work is always attended by BECOMING. Still there is work which is attended by BEING, as is, for instance, the writing of this.

Q: I still do not understand it completely, Baba. Isn't what I am doing now, this writing, also in the process of BECOMING since it hasn't been finished yet?

B: It is already there. The knowledge is there. You only write what you already know.

Q: But why then is, for instance, teaching a process of BECOMING?

B: Because it is not knowledge of the soul. The children are taught a cultivated knowledge, which they need for this life, not for the soul.

Q: So, what you need for this life is a process of BECOMING and what your soul needs all along is a process towards the state of BEING?

B: Yes, what your soul has known all along. That which is not acquired but on the contrary is revealed and which comes to the surface, whereas it was first hidden.

Q: Does peace of mind also have something to do with this?

B: Yes, everything. Only peace of mind goes further than bliss, beyond bliss is peace of mind. Inner peace is everlasting, is immortal. Bliss is the road

19

towards it. The last step, an encouragement.

Q: But bliss is so wonderful, why would anyone want to give that up?

B: Peace of mind is more wonderful still. You experience bliss through the contrast of non-bliss. Peace of mind is pure bliss but no longer experienced as such because, in a manner of speaking, non-bliss is also accepted as perfect happiness.

Q: Does bliss still have to do with ego and peace of mind doesn't anymore?

B: That is how it might be understood. Bliss still wants something. Peace of mind doesn't want anything anymore.

Q: I still would rather feel bliss than peace of mind at this moment.

B: That is because you know what bliss is, because peace of mind is not yet known to you, since there is no opposition there anymore and you can only understand things by their opposite.

5
RESISTANCE AND TIMING

11 May 1992

Following a dream in which Baba gives me repeated playful taps on the cheek, so that my head turns sideways and then comes back again. He does so ten times.

Question: Baba, why do You give me those taps on my cheek?

Baba: I want to see how much resistance is still there.

Q: That is quite a lot, is that bad?

B: No, a certain resistance is good. If there is no resistance, you would not be able to live. Your resistance is your individuality. If the resistance is too great, it is ego. If there is no resistance anymore, you merge in the spirit. The time hasn't yet come for that. You respond, but still return to yourself. The degree of tension and relief requires much care and attention. To the millimeter. It has to do with time. With "timing", to be more exact. Your timing makes you unique. The time which exists between tension and relief. There is only ONE timing which is as GOD wants it. When you have achieved it, you can progress. One's age has something to do with it.

Q: Why ten times?

B: Ten is the number of unity after having passed through the material world. In ten, God is one with man.

6
MAKING MISTAKES

17 August 1992

Question: Baba, how do I lose my ego?

Baba: Think of me at all times. There is nothing of which I am not the Doer. You only exist through my grace. If you are aware of that, how can you still have an ego? In everything you do, remember that it is not you, but I, who does it. I in you. Keep this always in mind. As soon as you forget this, your ego emerges again. The ego is necessary for this life on earth, but should be kept in check. Then it can become a partner in the spiritual process instead of an adversary. Then it contributes to making you aware at all times of your Divinity, of me in you. Know that I am there and that nothing happens which I have not willed. I am in everything. Everything is guided by me from within.

Q: Even when I make mistakes?

B: I gave you free will. With it you can make mistakes. As you live more consciously and let me be your guide, the less mistakes you will make, until finally you live faultlessly, that is to say sanctified.

Q: But, if everything is Your will, then our mistakes are also your will?

B: They are of no concern to me, your mistakes. I wait. Time is not important to me. Ultimately you will return to me and the time it will take is up to you. Through your mistakes you will have to suffer and your suffering will show you the way back to me. So, eventually it is I who has willed your mistakes.

Q: But mankind makes so many mistakes.

B: Mankind is like a rebellious horse. These are the last convulsions in quite a long process. A few lives more or less do not matter to me. All those countless lives as mineral, plant and animal, which preceded this life, have made man what he is today. One day he will come to me and then it will appear that time did not exist at all and that everything took place all at once.

Q: How can I understand that, Baba?

B: You cannot understand it. Just let it sink in and know that mistakes are made, because they must be made. They are part of the process. Know that with the growth of consciousness, making mistakes will diminish, for you as an individual, but also for the world. The earth has consciousness, just like every human being, and that consciousness is also in motion. As people on earth live more consciously, the greater the collective consciouness of the earth will become and the less mistakes will be made on earth. Then the earth will be sanctified.

Q: Will this be in the time of Prema Sai?

B: That time is nearer than you think.

7
THE PRONUNCIATION OF AUM

12 November 1992

During my meditation, in reference to an argument about the pronunciation of the AUM (or OM) mantra, Baba let me know:

Baba: The first part of the AUM-mantra is pronounced as one sound, the sound "OE". The word AUM consists of all the vowels, starting with the "A" as the first vowel, when the mouth is wide open, and ending with the "U" as the last vowel, just before the mouth is closed with the "M". Compare it to the colour white, which consists of all colours, yet is seen as one colour. In the same way the sound "AU", which consists of all vowels is pronounced in its totality as "OE". It is very good to concentrate on the colour white while reciting the mantra. AUM is white, is All. White is Light, is Love, is God.

8
TIME AND SPACE

16 January 1993

In pursuance of a rather strange sentence I heard during my meditation: "..., I have changed me with time".

Question: What do You mean by that?

Baba: All of life is one sequence of occurrences which together form one whole with time.

Q: Is time that important?

B: It is an essential part of matter. Without matter, no time; and without time, no matter.

Q: But isn't the material world an illusion?

B: Yes and no. Everything is an illusion when you experience unity. But, as long as this unity is not experienced, the material world is no illusion.

Q: Is there a reason for the fact that we live in the material world?

B: The reason is the material world itself.

Q: I don't understand.

B: The reason for matter is matter. Time and space are the reason for time and space.

Q: Baba, I do not understand, can you explain it differently?

B: There was a time in which time and space were One, in which God was One, in Himself. Through His unity, He created within Himself time and space.

Q: Baba, I do not understand and I really do not know whether I am making this up myself, or whether it is You, who writes through me.

B: When we live in time, we live in God; when we live in space, we live in God. When God lives in time and space, Maya (illusion) disappears. That is how God has willed it.

Q: What is it, then, that He has willed?

B: The cancellation of time and space through time and space. Then unity will be restored. We change with time. In the same way we change with space. Because of that, time and space change.

Q: What do you mean by we? Yourself as well, God?

B: Yes and no. That part of me that separated itself in matter (in time/space) changes along with Humanity. That part that created time/space can never change.

Q: So, it is again a question of thinking in terms of "and/and". One thing is true, and the other also?

B: Yes.

Q: Are we able to understand this with our intelligence, or is the intellect not the right means for it?

B: It can be understood; never with the intellect however, but... by experiencing it completely, through the integration of time and space in Man himself. He BECOMES time and space, or rather he IS time and space which has been given a form.

Q: But why the suffering?

B: Without suffering man would remain forever caught up in time/space. He would never be able to transcend it to experience the bliss of unity, for which he has been created. Suffering is unimportant in comparison with the eventual goal. It is necessary for the experience of that which transcends time/space.

Q: But why did You begin Creation, if that is where we have to go back to after lots of suffering?

B: Because I have to change with time. I have poured myself into Creation. I have separated myself in Creator and Creation, in order to change eventually as Creator.

Q: But why?

B: To give all of you the happiness of experiencing me. To give myself that happiness. Do you understand now how important it is for me that you all reach Me?

26

Q: Yes, our suffering must be terrible for You then.

B: When you people suffer, I suffer. Whatever you experience, I experience to a much greater degree. Your pain is my pain.

Q: But aren't You above pain and joy?

B: As Creator I know the outcome; as Creator time does not exist and therefore neither joy nor pain. As Creation I experience everything. I am each flower-bud which comes out. I am each tree which is cut. But, I am also the beautiful chest which is made of that wood and which perishes again. When Creator and Creation come together, unity has been reached. To me as Creator that unity is known, in me as Creation time is as much present as it is in you.

Q: Why are we, people with consciousness, different from the rest of nature?

B: In you, Creator and Creation come together. Eventually HE will be I.

9
POSITIVE AND NEGATIVE FORCE

22 February 1993

Question: Can You tell me something more about bliss (Your Ananda). Why do I feel it sometimes, but not always?

Baba: Only when my Self and yours overlap each other, do you live in bliss. Then this bliss will be permanent and you will not feel overwhelmed by it or be overfed by it. It is a blending of the "negative" and "positive" force. The positive force was there already. The negative force was still too weak; this force is developing until the negative pole achieves the same strength as the positive pole. When these two forces blend, the ego is free. The Force which is then released is radiant, clear, small and great at the same time and contains the whole cosmos. She lies rooted in each person. She was clearly defined at the beginning of time. Completion is at hand.

Q: For everyone?

B: For a large number of people, enough to carry the rest along. We do not need to wait for everyone, as long as their number is sufficient.

Q: What happens to the others?

B: God does not abandon anyone. Even when the negative pole is sufficiently strong, man's consciousness is not able to immediately support the power which is produced continuously. That power will be slowly increased. Only when the sub-conscious gets the upper hand, will it be possible for this Force to become entirely integrated. Then you will no longer experience it as something strange, coming from me and not from you, but as an essential part of yourself.

Q: Why is it that this Force is so often present during a bhajan-service?

B: That is the power of the gathering of many individuals. Then the positive pole becomes much more powerful because it isn't placed against the negative pole of one individual, but of many. Many who are opening themselves up to the positive pole. That is why bhajan-gatherings are important and, to an even greater extent, so are festivals. Because at a festival there are more individuals in the first place, and secondly, the individuals who are there are more receptive to the positive force.

Q: Is that what Jesus means when He says, "Where there are two or more in my name, I am present"?

B: Yes.

Q: And in the long run we don't need those bhajan-gatherings or festivals anymore to experience the positive force?

B: That is correct, but... only partly. You don't need them anymore to be able to experience the warmth and power, but you do need them to be able to send it out, to generate it in others. For, as has been said before, the more powerful and receptive the negative pole is, the stronger I can be present. Therefore everyone's process is also important to others. It is an interaction of individuals.

Q: If we are aware of this, doesn't our ego get inflated?

B: No, for as soon as the ego gets the upper hand, the power of the negative pole diminishes. And this is precisely the reason that the negative pole can only increase in strength if the ego decreases.

Q: I gather it all has to do with energy?

B: Everything is energy. Matter is energy. God is energy. Energy has been given a form to express Divinity. We are not only connected by energy, we ourselves ARE energy.

Q: And the source from which this energy comes is God?

B: Yes.

10
DIFFERENTIATION

16 May 1993

Following an incident that, according to Baba, has to do with the differentiation-process, as He calls it, which begins in our childhood.

Question: Do all characteristics, or rather character mechanisms that we acquire in our youth belong to the differentiation process?

Baba: Yes.

Q: So, it is through everything we experience that we develop into unique human beings, different from all others?

B: Yes.

Q: But what about the law of Karma?

B: Karma determines how the differentiation process will proceed. Because of Karma two people will always react differently to, and cope differently with, the same event.

Q: So, when something happens to us in our youth, it never is Karma?

B: Yes it is, for the opposite is also true. Something happens because of a certain Karma which needs to be worked out and the way one reacts to it advances the differentiation process.

Q: Why is this process so important?

B: Only when differentiation is optimal, will unity have been reached.

Q: You mean when everyone has become totally unique?

B: Yes.

Q: Is that why addiction to for instance drugs, alcohol or speed is so dangerous?

B: Yes, they weaken the differentiation process and slow you down on the way to unity.

Q: So, I developed a certain pattern of reactions in my youth, brought about by Karma, and now I use this in a differentiated stage?

B: Yes.

Q: But has the differentiation process ended then?

B: No, each moment you experience something new and the totality becomes different.

Q: Can I work on it myself?

B: Yes.

Q: How?

B: By going along with the stream. By letting me guide you. By responding with love to each person who treats you badly. By being sincere.

Q: Does Absolute Truth exist here on earth?

B: Yes, it does.

Q: Why do people deny it?

B: In their ignorance people may say that the absolute truth exists. This is dangerous. When people recognize the danger, they start denying this truth. At a higher level, however, when ignorance has been dispelled, Absolute Truth does exist. It is unalterable.

Baba's message becomes rather personal here. He ends this personal part by saying that it is only through loving one another that this truth can be made known.

Q: But what is to love exactly?

B: To love is everything. To live is to love, to breathe is to love, to be is to love.

Q: But then all of us love.

B: That is correct. Being on earth is an act of love. Man himself chose this existence out of love.

Q: But why do You say then that we must learn to love, that we have lost love?

B: Nothing else than that you must regain this understanding. That you must know again that you ARE love and that you have poured yourselves into existence out of love.

Q: Is knowing that we are love the same as knowing that we are God?

B: Yes.

Q: But is knowing this sufficient?

B: It is sufficient. However, it is not about intellectual knowledge, but about a totally integrated knowledge of one's entire being. Being permeated with love. To love oneself and know that one's love is sufficient in itself to give love to people. A conscious thinking-process need not enter into it.

Q: But why don't we recognize this love in each other?

B: It is that which keeps the world going. We do not need to recognize it in others, as long as we know, recognize, and acknowledge it in ourselves. Love is not a feeling in the sense that people give to it, like love for a husband, a wife, a child, work etc. Love is a state of BEING. It is a cooperation with God, in which He guides you and you comply with Him. The rest you leave to Him.

11
ABOUT THE ATTACK

8 June 1993

In pursuance of a dream, which I had on 4 June 1993 (!), in which four cats, among which my cat Kaya, try to harm Baba. Baba falls ill then and goes, supported by others, up a small staircase to the floor above. Later, when I hear about the attempted attack on Baba by four students which took place on 5 June 1993 (!), I connect the incident in my dream and the real event and I realize that cats are sweet, but all the same, unreliable. I also realize that actually the same applies to those four students, who all perished in the process. During the attack two of Baba's close assistants, who came forward to help Him, also lost their lives.

Question: Baba, did I understand this correctly ?

Baba: Yes. In your dream Baba also met with an "accident", didn't he? He triumphs but it is a question of identification.

Q: But wouldn't it be much easier for people to understand if nothing happens to Baba. He is God, so how can such things take place then? Baba, please answer me.

B: God has become Man and therefore He is subject to reality on earth. I will not let myself be taken away from you, but I will show you that I too can be in dangerous situations and that I am no different from you in that respect. This act presents at the same time a clear illustration of the distinction between good and bad. As Man among men, I am recognizable to many. They will feel pain for my sake. That pain is my pain, which I feel for the attackers' sake. The suffering must be assuaged. The identification must take effect completely. Those who think that God cannot let something like this happen and that therefore Baba is not God, do so entirely on their own responsibility. This says more about them than about me.
As Man I place myself among you and as Man I am vulnerable to accidents just as you are. Only they will not lead to catastrophe. You have no idea for how many people the incident is a relief. Many think, "See, He is not who He says He is," others respond in sorrow for my sake and find in it a purification

of their ego. There are only a few who have remained detached and who have relied on my Omnipotence and my Sankalpa. Becoming a human being means giving yourself completely to the earthly game, to as many people as possible at the same time, giving them what they want, not what you want, intervening only when things threaten to go wrong.

Q: And when lives are sacrificed in the process?

B: That is nothing new. It happens everywhere. They knew what they were in for when they took this birth.

Q: Is it an honour for them (those two close assistants) to die in this manner?

B: It certainly is, it has to do with the very highest redemption of Karma.

Q: And those four students? Did they also take birth for this specific purpose?

B: Yes, but that does not mean it can be condoned. It is a despicable act, which will pursue them during many lives.

Q: But if it had to happen?

B: The soul has a choice where this kind of incarnation is concerned. And that choice is completely free. It ties in with the game of life but it is a matter of free will if someone chooses to lend himself to it. No one will ever be forced, or is ever forced, to choose for evil.

Q: But what if it happens unconsciously, because the soul has not reached a sufficiently high level of consciousness yet?

B: Then also can we choose for good.

Q: But what about the law of Karma? For instance: When you are killed in a previous life, the one who killed you must suffer the same.

B: The other person will receive his lesson but it need not happen through you. This is precisely one of the ways to break through your Karma, to rise above feelings of hate and revenge.

Q: But why would a soul choose for evil, with all its consequences?

B: He does not choose, evil chooses him. At best he can say no.

Q: Why doesn't he say no then?

B: Because evil is stronger than he is, because evil has many different disguises and many seduction-manoeuvres.

Q: If that is the case, then it wasn't the person's fault in the first place.

B: Yes it was, whoever focuses on God will recognize evil at all times; only this is needed, this surrender to God.

Q: Does that mean that souls without a body have a possibility of choice, just as we have here on earth?

B: Yes, the difference lies in the gradation. The soul without a body chooses for the Whole, man on earth chooses for details.

Q: If a soul has made the choice for evil, can he still bring about changes in it when on earth?

B: It is difficult but it can be done. It is, in fact, the highest possible victory a soul can gain. That is another reason why souls may choose for evil. By accepting this challenge and then conquering it, souls will have disposed of a large part of negative Karma.

Q: So, if I understand correctly, there are two things at stake. 1. Everything is pre-ordained, good and evil; only, which soul chooses which role in life, is still open. 2. If a soul makes himself available for evil and then conquers that evil when on earth, in other words, when he does not go along with it, then that particular evil has been conquered in him?

B: That is correct.

Q: But doesn't that mean that everything was not pre-ordained?

B: Here we have a problem of the human intellect. For you it is either one thing or the other. But that both things can exist at the same time, as well as many more so-called contradictions, is not conceivable to you who live in duality . Since you live in duality, you always see either one facet or the other. But the totality, both facets existing at the same time and thus being neutralized, cannot be understood.

Q: Baba, I would like to know: does evil exist as an independent power, or has it also been created by You?

B: It has been created by me, but not as evil. Rather as a possibility of choice, in which the soul can plunge in order to conquer evil this way. And that is what always happens, everywhere.

Q: But it has gone on for so long!

B: It will go on much longer, because there will always be new souls who will have to make this choice. But if you realize that they are always different souls, it may be easier for you to accept.

Q: Except when the soul chooses for evil. In the Bible one can read about Judas, "It would have been better if this man had never been born" Is that true?

B: Yes, that is correct.

Q: But didn't someone have to take on that particular evil?

B: Then also the choice could have been made to overcome and undo that evil in himself.

Q: But then the entire story of Christ would have taken another course, wouldn't it?

B: Yes and no. On the earthly plane a slightly different plan would have been enacted. Another soul would, at another time, have committed himself to it. Souls need evil in order to grow. Think of a child. By falling it learns to keep his equilibrium.

Q: But many things are so atrocious.

B: They are not atrocious if you focus on God. Then everything is made light. All pain and sorrow, no matter how bad it may seem to others, is taken away from you. The only thing that remains is you and God, God and you. One bond of love.

12
HEALING POWER

4 August 1993

Following two Baba-dreams, right after my return from India, which among other things deal with female and male energy.

Question: Can You tell me about this female and male energy?

Baba: The divine positive force needs the negative pole to let the light shine. It is the female part in each human being to which this divine force appeals. In each human being the female part is as powerfully present as the male part. Only one is not aware of it. It is not the weak, the woman-imitating, unreal part in man (which both men and women display to a large extent), but the basic female force. The force of the earth. This force generates vibuthi. For vibuthi is also of the earth. The earth transformed by divine consciousness, so that only the very purest which can exist on earth remains. Vibuthi is the transformation of the basic female force by the divine creating force, until the essence remains, namely LOVE which comes from two sides and which always, at all times, works in a curative way. To work in a curative way it is of the utmost importance that one is aware of this female energy, which contains all of Creation. She is, as it were, an empty vessel which must be filled. But... an emptiness which has such a force that she draws everything towards herself. She fills herself with Prana (divine energy), whether she is aware of it or not. That way everything is always filled with divine energy, but at the same time she exists because of that energy. When one has become aware of this force, healing can be brought about. Healing power can start to flow through the person who has made a unity of the positive and the negative pole. And... healing power can work in a curative way for that person, in whom the negative pole is open, in other words, is recognizable.

Q: But aren't You the one who does everything?

B: Yes, everything is totally my will. Without my will nothing happens. However, it is my will to make love accessible to everyone. That is my great desire. Whoever wants to help me with it, I will help along.

Q: And if ego comes into play, the process would be stopped right away?

B: Yes, that is a natural law. Where there is ego the positive force will diminish and there will be disharmony. Positive and negative are no longer balanced then. All of Creation is filled with this basic female force, IS this force, exists by the grace of this force. It is important that you start to recognize it.

Following the continuation of the second dream, in which the number 6 appears, which, according to Baba, symbolizes the Shiva-power, and the number 3, which symbolizes Divinity.

Q: Baba, what is the difference between divinity and Shiva-power?

B: When the soul is no longer obscured by stains from and of the Kosas (protecting sheaths), the indwelling divinity can be brought out. Only then can the Shiva-power be put into operation. That power can only become really effective when there is a complete understanding of what one is doing. Divinity is an intuitive process of the heart, of a pure heart. Shiva-power is a process of the whole integrated consciousness, where all qualities and talents are used optimally, once the heart is pure and the nature sanctified.

Following a later continuation of this dream, in which there is talk of Baba on a swing. (Note that on special occasions Baba sits on a beautifully decorated swing. He says that this is how we should feel Him in our hearts, swinging gently back and forth.)

Q: Is there a connection between the transformation process of the earth and the swing with You on it, which we should feel in our hearts?

B: Yes and no. When I am sitting on the swing, I am indeed occupied with the transformation process, with the raising of the earth to heaven, but... when I am swinging in the heart, another process is going on. Then I bring heaven to earth, then there are no earthly ties anymore, to which the swing is connected. Then the heart is, as it were, being detached from earthly ties

13
NATURE

I am looking out of the window and trying to see the female force, the negative pole of which Baba spoke just now. It seems as if I begin to grasp a tiny bit of it. The plants, the grass, the trees, the wind, everything is so beautiful, so placid. Awaiting God, illuminated with God, in adoration of God. Is that the female force, this waiting, being, self-contained existence?

Question: Nature seems a good teacher. Are we like nature, with a few extra dimensions? Waiting, permeated with Divinity, in adoration of God, but not yet aware of it?

Baba: Yes. Nature is conscious of it, but at a plant level. Her consciousness is higher than that of an "unconsciously" living human being. A human being, however, who is aware of his Divinity, stands far above nature. He can make use of nature. He can cooperate with nature and impose his "Divine" will on nature. Never for his own sake - as soon as this happens the whole process will be disturbed and everything will have returned to its original state.

Q: It all requires so much attention, Baba!

B: No, that is not the case. It is rather a matter of complete trust, of completely knowing that it is like that and that it is not part of only one person, that each person has been created for this reason. This is not an intellectual process and it has nothing whatsoever to do with ego. It IS. And that is precisely what trust means. BEING, like that. Without restrictions, without fears, without thoughts. To act for love. Just like that, out of love for and solidarity with nature, of which man forms a part and which he has been placed above at the same time.

14

THE BHAJAN-SERVICE

8 August 1993

During the bhajan-service in our Sai Baba Centre in The Hague, I tried to understand what was going on. I often feel Ananda (bliss) in my heart there, which seems to have a connection with the bhajan-singing. "So, that is the female Shakti-energy," I thought. And then I suddenly understood, more or less, what is meant by: "I am the Word". The singing is, as it were, the positive force (see lesson 9) which is God, Him, Shiva, the Creator. The body that sings is the negative force, which is the earth, Shakti, Creation (of which both man and woman form part; men as well as women are female). The bhajans are the means of bringing Shakti (the negative pole) and SHIVA (the positive pole) together. This is the merging of God and man.

Question: Baba, have I understood correctly?

Baba: Yes.

Q: But if someone does not sing right from the heart, does what he sings remain Your Word just as well?

B: No, then it is hidden behind the ego. Not everything which is said or spoken on earth is my Word.

Q: So, only when someone sings completely free from ego, is it Your Word which is produced?

B: Yes.

Q: But how can it be that we sometimes have this feeling of bliss during the singing?

B: Then the positive and the negative force coincide.

Q: But that feeling of bliss is often more powerful during the communal singing than when I am singing bhajans at home by myself. Why is that?

B: Because the positive force which is present during a bhajan meeting is much stronger than at home.

Q: Does this mean that there are many people there who sing free from ego?

B: There are some, but that is not the point, for each effort to be free from ego reinforces the positive force. And even if my Word is not passed on optimally, the SHAKTI power (the negative pole, the female energy), on the other hand, is usually not optimally present either. However, in such cases the negative is the same as the positive and therefore my Love can flow unimpeded.

Q: But if I understand correctly, Love could flow much stronger still if the negative force was stronger, for then the positive force (coming from You through the singing) could also become stronger?

B: That goes without saying.

Q: How can the negative energy become stronger individually?

B: By living according to my teachings. By being pure and truthful. By enjoing BEING. By being part of creation.

Q: So, the singing is You in a greater or lesser degree?

B: Yes.

Q: And the songs that are sung?

B: As you already pointed out yourself, one of the means to reach me.

Q: Just as meditation and Seva (selfless help given to one's fellow-man) are?

B: Yes.

Q: And now You want us to start recognizing that female, negative force?

B: Yes.

Q: How?

B: By knowing that recognition is what it is all about. That the more consciously that force is lived and experienced, the more the divine consciousness can enter. It is a state of being completely receptive, empty. Then the attraction is so enormous that God must appear.

Q: But how can we recognize this in others?

B: You recognize it in the power of the singing. In the degree of silence. In the respect towards the other. In the devotion to your fellow man, for I am him. In the devotion to me. That I cannot resist. Only then is fully flowing love possible one hundred per cent.

Q: But You love us all equally?

B: That is because I know the future of each of you, and I know that eventually you will all come to me. If I adjust myself to perceiving things at an earthly level, I also adjust my flow of love accordingly.

Q: Does this often happen?

B: There is no difference. This life or the next is the same to me.

Q: But You free many people from fear and from their Karma from previous lives?

B: That does happen at the moment.

Q: Why?

B: Because in the Kali Yuga man has lost trace of the path in such a way that God's grace is bound to come into play. Mind you, only when man has first taken a step towards me.

Q: So, actually it is a great privilege to live in the Kali Yuga, because God's grace is more accessible than in other Yugas?

B: That is correct. However, that only applies to those who recognize and acknowledge God, those who live according to God's commandments and who sanctify God's name. No harm will touch them.

Q: Still, even these people are sometimes confronted with terrible things.

B: Then their faith in me was not strong enough. No harm will touch them. Watch my words. Harm may befall them, but they will remain untouched. I am with them and they are aware of it.

Q: This is how I understand it now:
. First a step is made towards God.
. God responds with love.
. Devotion is stimulated.
. God's love becomes stronger.
. The point is reached where through God's grace Karma is erased.
. Then one is able to become completely Divine. Equal to God.

B: When Karma has been erased, man is still able to build up new Karma. The degree to which he is conscious of it and allows it, determines the process of becoming Divine.

Q: So, when You have taken away old Karma this does not mean that at the same moment man is empty to such a degree as to receive You?

B: It only means that the possibility is offered to live towards the process of becoming divine without the burden of past lives.

Q: Is that what is meant by: "Jesus has died for our sins?"

B: It is exactly the same. Whoever gives himself to Jesus in complete devotion, recognizes this truth and knows that he is liberated. Then the process of sanctification can be put into operation.

Q: So, taking away one's Karma is the same as forgiving one's sins?

B: Yes.

15

PLEASURE-SEEKING

9 August 1993

Following a dream in which Baba shows me that we must strive for equanimity; that that part in us which seeks pleasure (represented in the dream by a male Guru) must be banished.

Question: There is something which I do not understand, Baba. Does that part in us which seeks pleasure have to do with the male energy?

Baba: Yes, of course. God seeks fulfilment and pleasure; only... divine pleasure, bliss, Ananda. When this search takes place subconsciously, it is projected towards earthly (= transitory) pleasures and precisely because of that the road towards divine pleasure is obstructed. However, striving for pleasure is a process of the male (positive) energy. The female (negative) energy is only receptive, empty, without any wishes or desires. It is always the positive force present (that which is still vaguely aware of its Divinity), which creates the longing and desire for things. Then it enters into an unreal combination with the female negative force, which subsequently, at a subconscious level, thinks that it is filled with that for which it has been created. A Karmic bondage of illusion arises, which can last thousands of lives. The female is no longer totally receptive, the male no longer seeks the very highest. This must be undone and for this, devotion is the best medium. For devotion is a combination (at a subconscious level) of the highest possible female receptivity and the highest possible male pleasure-seeking, until the devotion has increased to such a degree that God appears.

Q: But isn't devotion by itself grace already?

B: Devotion knows many stages. The first steps on the path of devotion are often made after a period of total hopelessness. (That in fact everything is God's grace, is only understood much later). Devotion is then the only solution. Surrender as it were. God's grace responds and in that way the process can continue. If God's grace is recognised/acknowledged, the process will be expedited. If that doesn't happen, many more lives can be spent in this half divine/half human state. In each stage anew recognition/acknowledgement is necessary or else the process will stop.

Q: Is a relapse also possible?

B: Yes, that happens. Not often though, and often only temporarily. The person who has once tasted divine pleasure - no matter how little - will no longer be easily satisfied with its absence. He is, as it were, able to make a comparison - often subconsciously.

Q: So, pleasure-seeking on earth - no matter in what form - is the divine which at a subconscious level is vaguely aware of its divinity and which is longing to have it return?

B: Yes.

Q: But it deteriorates so enormously here on earth.

B: That has to do with the complications of Karma and with the fact that only after having experienced the worst is man really prepared to travel the road to God. These are fundamental laws, which man must comply with when he has turned away from God.

Q: So, the divine longing - the male energy, God himself - can totally turn away from God?

B: Yes, the search for God can end up at the opposite pole, evil.

Q: But that means that God ends up at evil?

B: Evil is part of God. It is God not recognized as such and necessarily transformed into evil.

Q: So, it does not really exist?

B: It exists as long as man turns away from God.

Q: Which means as long as God turns away from God, since it is the male energy?

B: Yes, as long as an aspect of God is not aware of the fact that it is God.

16
A HUMAN BEING HAS FREE WILL

7 November 1993

Following a personal message in which there are two scenarios between which Baba is hesitating.

Question: How is it that You, as God, still hesitate between two scenarios?

Baba: Man has free will. Governments, Boards of directors etc. also have free will. Making plans and working them out belongs to a person's free will. As long as the things which are being worked out are not contrary to the divine plan, I let people have their "relative" freedom to work out plans as they think fit. This concerns comparatively small choices, with comparatively small consequences, even though they may seem very great to the person concerned.

Q: But don't You, as God, know the outcome?

B: I know the final outcome. I could know the comparatively less important details, if I focus on them, but since I don't, you could say that I don't know them. Or rather: I so choose because I choose to leave it up to a person to make his own decision. Only when things threaten to go totally wrong, and only if there are no other possibilities of solving the problem, do I interfere.

Q: And in the case of wars? Like the First and Second World War, and now Yugoslavia? Isn't it a fact that You don't interfere there either?

B: I don't interfere collectively, but I do individually. The collective crystallization of evil must proceed in cases of war and natural disasters. But at an individual level people are certainly helped. And don't forget that whoever finds himself in such a situation, has to resolve a specific Karma. No birth has taken place without a reason. One is placed where the law of Karma must be accomplished.

Q: But why is it then that sometimes You do interfere individually?

B: My grace can cancel out the law of Karma, and this is put in action as soon as a person surrenders to me. Then his fate will be in my hands and he can be protected from any violence. Mind you, he *can* be protected, but his life will not necessarily be saved. Something will be made clear to him about the divine consciousness though, which will give him a good basis for development in a next life, in case there is no longer any need to keep him in this life.

Q: As in the case of Mrs. X? I and many others have prayed to You to help her and still her health is deteriorating continuously. Despite the vibuthi we give her and despite our prayers. How can that be? Does that mean that our prayers are without any effect, or were they not intense enough?

B: Praying is not done for the result, neither is giving vibuthi. Continue praying and giving vibuthi, leave the result to me. My blessing rests on the reason why this has to happen. You must trust that prayers are not for nothing. Keep praying for her, but don't expect anything. "Miracles" should not be expected. They happen unexpectedly, that is the essence of a miracle. I know how, when and for whom I will come into action and I also know why this apparently sometimes does not happen. Ask her if she trusts me. Her answer will be an unqualified "yes". At a deeper level she knows why this is happening to her and she acquiesces in her fate. Her "gain" is great, which she also knows. By turning to me in these difficult circumstances, she has gained a great deal. It is precisely this not knowing consciously and still trusting, which brings a person closer to God. I take care of her and her kin and she knows this with an inner knowledge. That is why she is able to bear what is happening to her.

17
COMPLETE TRUST IN BABA

7 November 1993

Following a personal message in which Baba speaks about trust in Him and the lack of it. He compares this trust to a stream. The greater the trust, the more He can work with us and through us.

Question: Do many people have this lack of trust?

Baba: Yes, as long as the stream does not flow quickly, this is no problem. God is not worried about a few lives more or less. But, once the stream picks up speed, everything goes very rapidly. There is no stopping it anymore. It is all or nothing. Solid banks are needed then to confine the river. Then you need my total guidance. Where trust is complete, my guidance will also be complete. Just as in the case of the river there is a natural passage for the rapids. And where there is none, the river will form one herself. The same holds true for man. When his life is fully focused on God, there is an interaction between him and God. Man turns to God as his guide and God cannot but guide him. In that way man forms, as it were, his own banks. Because of the fact that he turns to God, God turns to him. Nothing can go wrong then. He is guided, provided that the acceleration proceeds in a regular and natural manner. Should too much water want to flow at the same time, the banks will not hold it, new banks must be formed then. This takes time. To prevent this, it is I, who regulates the acceleration process.

Q: But time doesn't exist?

B: In the material world we have to take account of time. Time exists where there is matter. Time no longer exists, when matter has been conquered. Until then man is trapped in time and I bear that in mind when guiding him. When a river starts picking up speed - in other words, when the end of the stream of many, many lives is in sight - the process of time plays a significant part. Each minute requires much care and attention, man cannot afford to waste time then. Should this threaten to happen, I interfere.

18
THE INTERMEDIATE STAGE

17 December 1993

Following a problem which keeps cropping up: Baba wants us to know that we are God, that we are divine creatures. Now imagine that one starts to recognize this in oneself and therefore starts to see things more purely and then, precisely because of it, realizes that others do not (yet) recognize this in themselves, because of the mistakes they make. Doesn't one place oneself above them then and is that not an enormous ego-trap?

Question: How is that, Baba? Please give me an answer to this.

Baba: It is different.

Q: How then?

B: It is an intermediate stage.

Q: Whàt is an intermediate stage?

B: Knowing that you are God is the intermediate stage. The final stage is BEING God, in all humility and loving all because you know that they too are God, only they are not yet aware of it.

Q: So, if you are not yet aware of it, you make mistakes?

B: Even if you are aware of it, you make mistakes. That is not the point.

Q: Then what is the point?

B: What is important is that attention is paid to everything. That prevents a person from making mistakes, but it also results in a clearer recognition of the mistakes of others. That is the intermediate stage, as it were. What you do is this: you are making use of the differentiation process to arrive at a divine consciousness. During the process, there will be stages in which things coincide which are actually not comparable. The ability of being able to see facts purely is to enjoy what the earth has to offer, not to judge when things are not yet completely purified.

Q: But isn't it precisely then that you see and hear the mistakes of others much more clearly?

B: People should ignore that. They should not use their newly acquired talent for it. They should focus their attention on the whole, not on details. With this purity they should try to experience unity and not become even more involved in diversity.

Q: So, when we are finally able to say of ourselves, "I am God," we should not use this to study unrelated things or people, but to experience unity?

B: Yes.

Q: But isn't that terribly difficult at such a moment, just when all those unrelated facts are being outlined so clearly?

B: That is why it is an intermediate stage. Eventually it will not be difficult. The degree of purity, in which things and people are seen without faults, is necessary to start experiencing the consciousness of unity. One should look past other peoples' mistakes, one should look at who they really are, knowing that they form part of that unity, that I work through them.

Q: Even if they make mistakes?

B: That is part of the Divine play. Mistakes are made to be learned from. Both he who makes them and he who observes them learn from them.

19

ILLUSION

4 February 1994

Question: Baba, why do we have to be born into the material world to experience everything?

Baba: When you dream you also think that you are in the material world.

Q: So, this is not the material world at all?

B: Yes and no. As long as you are in it, it is the material world, just as in the dream.

Q: Baba, in my dreams I may dream about a certain person, but such a person often symbolizes a part within myself. Does the same hold true for life in the material world, in our reality?

B: Yes.

Q: But still, that person, who functions as a symbol for a certain quality in myself, also exists in real life. He lives a real life, unknown to my dream. How can that be?

B: In the waking-consciousness too, the other person plays a symbolic role towards you and has at the same time his own life unknown to you, while still others have a symbolic function towards him, without your intellect being aware of it.

Q: But is the Self aware of it?

B: The Self does not know anything, but IS everything. The Self is not in need of knowing, only of BEING.

Q: But You know everything, of everyone.

B: The Self has completely manifested in me. I and the Self are one. That is why I am all that lives and all that is animated, and all that IS.

Q: But do You also serve as a symbol then?

51

B: My form here on earth serves as a symbol for this Self. The Self is not the form. The Self is everywhere, all-pervading. I am everywhere, all-pervading. My form is only temporary, bound to time, just as any form is. What remains, is what IS, what always was and what always will be. In that respect there is no difference between you and me, between you and everyone or everything else.

Q: But why do we live on earth then?

B: To become completely conscious of BEING. To BE completely conscious.

Q: But if everything has always been there already, why was there a need for it?

B: Consciousness was only known to itself. It separated from itself to make itself known.

Q: To whom?

B: Just to make itself known. To become visible in the game of creation.

Q: But why?

B: There is no Why. It is as it is. There is only a because (BE CAUSE!). The causal, **that** from which everything has been created. (The causal **THAT**, from which everything has been created).

Q: You want us to know that we are God, but how can we know it, if we cannot, like You, look into everyone and be everyone?

B: Look into your Self, be your Self, then you are in everyone.

Q: I cannot say that everything is suddenly clear to me now, Baba.

B: That is beside the point.

Q: What is the point then?

B: To go on completing what you were born for. The act of entering into a form - a seeming form, mind you -is one of surrender, of love. Complete it with the means that are at your disposal: your senses, your intellect, your circumstances, your talents. Work towards perfection. If you are perfect, the world is perfect - over and over again. Each human being is a new creation, or rather is a creation in itself. In its Self.

Q: But what about the interaction?

B: Nothing exists unrelated to the other and yet everything IS the other. That is what is meant by unity.

Q: Do You actually want us to understand? Knowledge is important, isn't it?

B: What happens - not what I want - what happens is that knowledge comes from within as a condition of BEING, an inner knowledge, for which no intellect is needed.

Q: Can we still talk about it then or should we just smile and be silent?

B: The latter. Speaking is no longer necessary then.

Q: But of what benefit is that to others?

B: Is that important?

Q: I think it is.

B: Others will come to the source, which they themselves are. They can draw from that source if they are thirsty, or they can leave it, just knowing that the source is there in case they are thirsty. It provides security, security for their existence. It makes it easy to go on'living, to complete their lives.

Q: Is that what we are to each other?

B: What we could eventually be to each other.

Q: Will the time come when everything is so completely One, so stilled?

B: Yes.

Q: For everyone at the same time?

B: No.

Q: But then that time will never come.

B: Whoever has arrived at that stage experiences the world likewise. Then there is no difference anymore.

Q: And for the Self?

B: The Self does not experience any difference between now, then or before. The Self IS that stilled Oneness.

Q: Does the Self manifest itself through love?

B: Yes.

Q: And through truth?

B: Truth is an expression of love.

Q: And is love an expression of the Self?

B: No, love IS the Self.

Q: So, now as Sathya Sai You are an expression of love (Sathya means truth) and before long, as Prema Sai, You will be love itself?

B: Yes.

Q: Is there a difference?

B: Not as far as I am concerned; yes, as far as people are concerned. As Sathya Sai only those people can experience my love, who are open to receive it, who acknowledge the truth of it. As Prema Sai there is no stopping it anymore, everything and everyone will be bathed in love, will experience that love.

Q: But around me I see people, who acknowledge You, but who do not really live in truth.

B: They experience my love-stream to the extent in which they live in truth. It cannot be otherwise. The more a person stands erect in truth, the more he really IS, the more he experiences me. If despite his shortcomings he still acknowledges me, it is a process, a step on the way towards truth.

Q: And when you are Prema Sai, this will be no longer necessary? Your love will then be experienced by everyone in equal measure?

B: If someone is still only on the way and does not yet completely live in truth, my love will be so overwhelming that truth will follow of its own accord. Beholding me will then immediately complete the process.

Q: So, people do indeed need to see You in the form?

B: People need to see me and to know that they are being seen by me. That does not need to take place per se in the form. Neither now nor then.

Q: But it is for many the only way to continue growing quickly, isn't it?

B: Yes, most need it. Only those who have already transcended the form, can see me and experience me wherever they are.

Q: Are they all conscious of it?

B: They are conscious of Good, not necessarily of God. They are whole, therefore good, therefore God.

Q: Are there many of them?

B: There are very few. Most should come to me.

Q: And what about animals?

B: An animal is an extension of a human being. Man takes the animal along with himself. An animal is a reflection of what man used to be at one time. An obsolete form, as it were, of what man once was.

Q: But isn't the animal also itself?

B: The Self is also manifest in the animal and that is essentially different.

Q: But isn't an animal capable, from rebirth to rebirth, of becoming Man and then God?

B: Yes. But that can also have taken place already.

Q: I don't understand, could You explain it?

B: The animal can, complete in itself, BE already. Only fulfilling that for which it IS, in order to then merge into BEING again, without having to be reborn. A soul which is destined to become a human being can choose to be an animal and evolve from there.

Q: When I spoke about animals I actually meant those countless mosquitos, fleas, insects, germs, etc. I did not mean pets. Was Your answer also given in that context?

B: Yes.

Q: So, it is not necessary for all those living things to go all the way towards becoming man with everything that entails?

B: No.

Q: That explains a lot to me, for if all those living creatures would each individually have to become human beings....! Still, isn't it true that all those masses, those countless little animals are also permeated with the Atma, how is that possible?

B: The Atma, the Self, pervades everything, also that which does not live; each molecule, atom, subatom is permeated with the Self.

55

Q: But isn't the Atma that which evolves until and beyond having become Man?

B: The Atma IS, it does not evolve.

Q: What is it that evolves then?

B: Consciousness. Being conscious of the Self.

Q: And for instance a mosquito, isn't conscious of it?

B: A mosquito is a mosquito.

Q: And a mosquito which bites me, does it function as a symbol for something in myself which is being bitten?

B: Yes.

Q: But what or who moves that mosquito to perform that symbolic act?

B: The Self.

Q: But the Self is unchangeable, isn't it?

B: It is all One, everything has happened already. Oneness includes Present, Past and Future. The interaction between you and that mosquito is the same as between you and others.

Q: A soul destined to become Man, can never incarnate into a mosquito?

B: Yes, it can. But.... not every mosquito harbours a soul destined to become a human being. That is the difference.

Q: Then what is the use of all those mosquitos? Are there so many of them to enable that particular mosquito to eventually become Man?

B: They form part of nature, which forms a unity.

Q: Do we as people also form part of nature?

B: Nature can do without man, man cannot do without nature.

Q: And if nature is hostile to us?

B: She is only hostile as long as man is his own inner enemy.

Q: So, when man IS, when he no longer BECOMES, when he has reached Oneness, he will no longer be bothered by, for example, a mosquito?

B: He can still be bitten, but he will thank the mosquito for it.

Q: Because it has taught him a lesson?

B: Among other things.

Q: But he didn't need to learn anything anymore. Hadn't he already arrived at his goal?

B: He is thankful because he has served as a food-source for the mosquito.

Q: So, he does not ask himself if there was something in him which had to be bitten, or let itself be bitten?

B: A realised person does not ask himself anything, he IS and accepts. He loves and radiates this love.

Q: And pets, Baba, do they harbour souls which will once be human beings?

B: Most of them do.

Q: Not all?

B: No.

Q: Have some of them already been man once?

B: Yes, that also happens.

Q: Is it a relapse then?

B: Sometimes it is, sometimes it isn't. It can be a necessary lesson, without having to be a relapse.

Q: There is still something I don't understand: if everything is a dream, is not really there, then what about reincarnation, Karma, animals?

B: They form part of that dream.

Q: So, they do not really exist?

B: Nothing really exists.

Q: But an animal cannot dream itself, can it?

B: Neither can man. The only thing which creates the dream is the Self. And... an animal is itself. Is its Self. Is IT.

Q: Somewhere you have said that an animal is only 20% God, and a human being is 80% God. How am I to understand that in this context?

B: God is not an animal. An animal functions as a symbol for that above which man should rise. In that context the animal is hardly God. As part of creation, which is One and an illusion, the animal forms as much part of that Oneness as anything else that exists.

20
ONENESS

13 February 1994

Following a special experience, in which I became suddenly very strongly aware of the interconnection of everyone. I saw myself in everyone and was able to experience "my soul is everyone's, the body functions as a sheath, there is no difference". I looked, as it were, from the Atma within me at the Atma within everybody else. When I ask Baba for an explanation, He gives among other things the following answer:

Baba: The point is that body-consciousness and Atma-consciousness become one. Atma and body are to form one whole. There will be no more discrepancy.

Question: And then we cannot fall ill any longer?

B: Yes, you can.

Q: Does that imply that the Atma becomes ill, isn't that impossible?

B: It implies that the Atma chooses to undergo a certain illness.

Q: Why should the Atma choose to do so?

B: There are several reasons. One obvious reason is: To take upon oneself a part of someone else's Karmic debt.

Q: And one's own Karmic debt?

B: One's own Karma will have been erased then.

Q: What are the other reasons?

B: Experiencing the illness in order to conquer it that way.

Q: That specific disease?

B: Yes, or an aspect of it.

Q: Is that the reason why Ramakrishna died of cancer of the throat?

B: Yes.

Q: But cancer of the throat still exists.

B: It has to be worked out in time. Ramakrishna, however, did conquer throat-cancer.

Q: Did he choose to do so voluntarily?

B: It was not a question of choosing, there was no choice anymore. Things were as they were.

Q: But he did have to suffer.

B: Suffering is nothing. For him suffering was nothing. A matter of minor importance. It hardly touched him.

Q: Did this also hold true for Christ?

B: Christ went consciously as Man through the suffering. He experienced the suffering at the level of humanity. That made his suffering an awe-inspiring sacrifice. He only had to ask for exemption, and immediately it would have been taken away from Him.

Q: But then many people would have had to endure much more difficult Karmas still?

B: That is correct. His suffering has cleared the way towards me for many and is still doing so.

Q: Even if they do not know You?

B: They know God, the form is of no importance.

Q: So, there is a difference between Ramakrishna and Christ?

B: Christ WAS. Ramakrishna had to BECOME.

Q: And You ARE?

B: Yes, I AM from aeon to aeon. Christ WAS in time.

Q: In the book "When God walks the earth", by Jack Shemesh, it is written that Christ has come back to earth in order to merge in Prema Sai. Is that true?

B: Yes.

Q: Will He be recognized?

B: By many.

Q: When?

B: In thirty years.

Q: Will the Christians see Him then as the second coming?

B: No, not as such.

Q: Will Prema Sai be seen as the second coming?

B: Yes.

21
"I"-CONSCIOUSNESS

20 February 1994

During this morning's bhajan-service in the Sai Baba-Centre in the Hague something happened which seems like a continuation of the previous experience. Suddenly there was no "I" at all anymore, there was only "THAT". THAT was the Atma experience, the experience of bliss. THAT was all there was, nothing else, no body, nothing. I could think it over and yet there was no "I" anymore. How that is possible, I do not know, but it did happen. Now, back at home, the Atma experience of bliss is still there, but at the same time I am myself again, with my own "I". What then is the difference?

Question: Baba, will You let me know, please? Is there a difference?

Baba: Yes and no. There is a difference, because that is what you feel, but essentially there is never any difference. Objectively there is actually no "I" at all. And you entered into that objectivity. Now you are back in subjectivity again and experience the "I"-feeling once more.

Q: Is that the same as ego?

B: Ego and "I"-consciousness do not entirely overlap. As long as you live, you will regularly experience the "I"-consciousness. You would not be able to function on earth otherwise. The ego, at least that what is understood by ego, is knowledge of this "I"-consciousness and projection of it on worldly things.

Q: And that is wrong?

B: Not always, but often it is. When your "I"-consciousness makes use of things as they come in handy, and then lets go of them again when their momentary function is no longer needed, it is ego put to the right use. When your "I"-consciousness gives an interpretation to things out of ignorance and acts accordingly, it is a projection of the ego and therefore not right.

Q: So, in duality we live with our soul in the "I"-consciousness and when that consciousness just uses things and then lets go of them, there is no problem, but when it starts colouring things, then it becomes ego?

B: That's right. It is not only about "using" and about "things". It is also about communicating and about people. Interaction is necessary. With it the world is kept going. But, that is all it is. For there is no difference in fact. Therefore, as soon as interaction is coloured through all kinds of projections, we start applying differences.

Q: But what about differentiation? Aren't we all different from each other?

B: We complete each other. In that way we form a unity, not only where the Atma is concerned but also in the material world. In the Atma, in other words at soul-level, the One has separated itself into diversity. In the material world - at a physical level - all diversity forms the One.

Q: And then body and soul will be one?

B: Eventually they will.

Q: Does this hold true for the whole earth?

B: It holds true for everyone who experiences it. It is the experience of a fundamental idea which exists already but is not experienced as such.

Q: What has bliss got to do with it?

B: Bliss or Ananda is the Atma which is conscious of itself.

Q: And peace of mind? (see lesson 4)

B: Peace of mind is complete unity, where there are no contradictions anymore.

Q: Just as when I knew during the bhajan-service this morning, there is no "I"?

B: Yes.

Q: Yet I knew of my existence, how is that possible?

B: It is possible, you experienced it, let that be the proof of it.

Q: Does it go further still?

B: It can manifest itself anywhere and in all kinds of situations, and eventually it will be completely integrated.

Q: Do you then always live feeling: there is no "I" ?

B: Yes. Then everything will be one and the same.

Q: And still one functions as if there were an "I"? Just like during the service? I was just sitting there and I am convinced that to the others I was exactly the same as I always am.

B: Precisely, that is what it is all about, you ARE, One without a Second.

Q: It is like You walking in Puttaparthi. You are the Atma that walks there. At the same time You say, "There is no difference". Still You are there in a form, separate from us. Is that it?

B: I experience myself as you, because the form is not what it is all about. The form is of secondary importance. A casual circumstance, you could call it. Temporary and replacable.

Q: And yet, You came to us in the form, in Your specific form. Then shouldn't that form serve some purpose?

B: Of course. As was said before, the form serves as an interactive medium, to keep the world going. In the form differentiation exists and everyone plays his own role in it.

Q: So, You play the role of Avatar?

B: Not quite. In the case of an Avatar, and of each fully realised human being, Atma and form coincide; together they form One.

Q: But isn't an Avatar different from a fully realized human being?

B: The difference lies in the fact that an Avatar is born as such, with all the knowledge at hand. A realized human being has acquired it during the course of his life on earth.

Q: So, soul and form having to become One is what life here on earth is all about?

B: Yes.

Q: I think I am starting to understand it a little. Therefore the question that I was struggling with (see chapter 18), whether people should realize all at the same time that soul and form are One, so that the earth can really elevate itself, is absolutely out of order at such a moment, for there is no "I", no separate self, at all. So, that thought is totally irrelevant?

B: That is correct.

Q: But what about the "I"-consciousness then?

B: There is no ego then, no "I". There is an "I"-consciousness though, that comes from the Atma. The Atma overlaps the form and form and Atma together constitute the "I"-consciousness. So, there is no "I", there is only "THAT", the Self and the body united.

Q: Baba, is there more?

B: Yes, there is more. You should know that all is animated and lives from within. That what lives exists through the Atma from within. That what comes from without is added and therefore prone to pollution. Remove that pollution and the Atma is revealed.

Q: But Baba, for another person we are also that which comes from without, aren't we?

B: For ourselves too we are that which comes from without. Only when the Atma is experienced, nothing comes from without anymore, neither you nor the other.

Q: What exactly do You mean by "from without"?

B: Everything that is illusion, everything that exists in the world of duality.

Q: You mean the material world?

B: Not quite, when the material world has been consciously animated from within, duality does no longer exist, despite the fact that it is still the material world.

Q: As in Your case?

B: Yes, I am One. The Atma and the form are One, animated from within.

Q: Yet You say that the form is not important.

B: The form is in the process of being transformed or has already been transformed and in doing so the Atma has created itself as form. Even if the form would be dissolved again, it will also at all times keep on existing as form for whoever calls on it, or to whosoever it wishes to reveal itself.

Q: Just as for instance Krishna or Jesus also still exist as form?

B: That's right.

Q: Before You existed as the form of Sai Baba, was the appearance to others not possible in that form?

B: Exactly, that is the importance of the "divinised" form. Once it has manifested itself, it will be there as long as the earth lasts.

Q: Are saints divinised forms as well?

B: Some of the saints are. Those who chose to be so.

Q: Mary for example?

B: Yes, she is a divinised form, who is, through the form, able to act as an intermediary between people and God.

Q: Not all saints are?

B: No, some have merged in God, without having to perform another task on earth. Both Atma and form have merged in God. With others it is the Atma that has merged, whereas the form is still able to manifest itself on earth. Others again manifest themselves, Atma and form, on earth.

Q: Like You?

B: I am the totality of all forms, the divinised as well as those that still have to become divinised. In me it merges. In me everything will eventually merge.

Q: Then there will be nothing anymore?

B: Then there will be everything.

22
DO NOT JUDGE

6 March 1994

Following an incident in which I saw that another person was being treated wrongly and I tried to intervene.

Baba: Leave things as they are. Do not try to take a stand when you have nothing to do with the incident, when it does not concern you.

Question: Not even when I see that someone is being treated unjustly?

B: Not even then. What you see as an injustice could well be something quite different. Nothing happens without my will. Neither does the "seeming" injustice. If it takes place and you see it but it does not concern you, just let it happen.

Q: But if, for instance, a child is being maltreated in front of my eyes?

B: That is a different matter. Each incident is complete in itself and one should respond adequately in each case. Just now I was talking of injustice which cannot or will not be changed in any way by your intervention. Besides, in the long run the child will probably not be better off by your intervention either. Chances are that it may even have an inverse effect on the one who is maltreating, in so far that he might treat the child worse later on.

Q: But isn't it true that we have to take action, Baba?

B: Yes and no. Yes, when it is really as obvious as you just sketched. Most of the time things are not that obvious. No, if things are not obvious enough for you to be able to envisage the whole. Focus on me at all times. Let me be your guide. I decide when intervention must take place. Leave these matters to me.

Q: I cannot imagine that one should not be allowed to help in the case of cruel injustice.

B: Let whatever happens, happen. A person is confronted with things, when it is necessary for him to take action. If it is not necessary, such things will not present themselves. And if they should occur, then again, each incident requires adequate action at that moment of time and for that specific case.

Q: But isn't it good to think of things in advance and draw up a plan to do something in case that... ?

B: As far as it concerns yourself there is nothing wrong with doing that, but where it concerns others, who are otherwise not in a position to affect your path, it is never allowed. That would come down to taking upon yourself the path another has to travel and no one but I can do that. Keep that in mind when in similar circumstances you might get the idea that you ought to take action.

Q: Does that hold true for everyone?

B: Yes, always and everywhere.

Q: So, taking sides is out of the question?

B: Unless one has to literally take sides (in case of elections). In all other cases it is not good. Consider everything with equanimity, do not let yourself be swept along by this or that. Choose the Middle Path. See and do not judge. God judges, not Man.

Q: As is written in the Bible, "Judge not, that you may not be judged".

B: That is correct.

Q: Not even when the case is very clear?

B: Not even then. Definitely not when it is unasked for. Someone may ask to be helped in taking a decision. That is another matter, then you are allowed to help. But also then caution and great integrity should be exercised. The path of Dharma is not always the easiest path, all the same, it is the path which should at all times be pointed out to the other. Keep unwavering in that respect.

Q: And if it is You who lets a person walk another path?

B: How can I ever let someone walk a path other than that of Dharma?

Q: But if somebody says that it is You who wants it that way, that it is You who speaks through him, or that he receives images that You give to him. What should I choose then - what the other says or that which I see as the path of Dharma?

B: Always follow your own interpretation.

Q: And if the other does not listen to it?

B: Then it is not your business anymore.

Q: But isn't it You then, who speaks through the other, or who gives him advice?

B: Yes, it is I, but a misinterpretation in the other person's favour is always possible and creeps in quickly. That is one of the reasons that I do not readily present myself in such a manner to people. The things one "sees", are seen in images; they come from the mind with all its restrictions.

Q: What exactly is the mind? It does not quite cover our thoughts, does it?

B: The mind encompasses those thoughts which exist independently without Man having a grip on them. It also encompasses the thoughts which a person can control. One should transcend both. The latter, namely transcending thoughts which man evokes himself, is easier than the former, namely transcending involuntary thoughts of which one is unaware. There also lies the treacherous side of visions, which are regarded as being independent of Man. That is partly true, but they are always coloured by the human capacity for understanding. It is advisable to be alert in matters like this. Especially so when it concerns another person and it isn't within your experience. You need never go along with it. Even if the other says that it is I whom he sees or who speaks through him. Do you experience it that way? No? Then it does not hold true for you. Test everything against your own code of conduct, against your own conscience and against the path of Dharma as you understand it.

Q: And if I interpret it incorrectly?

B: The purer your life, the less easy it is to misinterpret Truth. There are some things which are incontestible, which cannot be departed from. You will recognize them more and more.

Q: Sometimes You let things happen, which I think should not happen according to the law of Dharma. For instance when a devotee of Yours gets a divorce. That can't be called Dharmic, can it?

B: It isn't Dharmic, especially not when it is brought about by Man. It is another matter when I let it happen. Things take place the way I want them to happen. Man, who has to walk the path of Dharma, is set aside then. My will will be carried out. It only remains for man to travel the path of Dharma in the renewed circumstances.

23
DESIRES

8 March 1994

Question: Baba, what about this? People say that they communicate with You. They receive Your personal messages for practical use. Sometimes they come true, but then again sometimes they don't. How is that possible?

Baba: That is a matter of misinterpretation.

Q: But when You say "yes" in answer to a question, how can that be misinterpreted?

B: What happens is that when a person still has certain desires, I reflect back to him what he desires. Then, if that does not come true, he is confronted with his own desires. As long as there is still desire, that person is not pure and I cannot speak clearly through him to him. Only when there are no longer any desires, will I be able to communicate clearly and be optimally understood. Now, if a person has a desire and asks me to fulfill it within a certain, measurable period of time, I will assent. In fact it is not I who assents, but his own imperfection. When time has passed and that which he thinks to have heard from me, or which he thinks has been affirmed by me, has not come true, he will start doubting me. One step further goes he who starts doubting himself. One more step goes he who realizes, that he prevents me from being a clear guide because of his desire for this or that. When a person is not pure, he will never be able to "hear" me clearly.

Q: But I am now talking about people who do not so much ask anything for themselves, but rather for another.

B: As long as there is a subconscious desire to receive assurance, a person's trust in me is not great enough and therefore what I give to him is a reflection of his own lack of trust.

Q: But isn't that very confusing? Wouldn't his lack of trust only diminish that way?

B: Not as soon as people realize that this happens. When they are aware of it, they know that each desire, whether it is for themselves or for someone else, keeps me away from them to a greater or lesser extent.

Q: But aren't we allowed to ask for anything then?

B: You may ask anything, but you should expect nothing. If a person asks without insistence, if the request is placed in the manner of, "Swami, this is what I would like, but when You have something else in mind for me, that is all right too, I will accept that equally well", then communication between this person and me is much purer and success is guaranteed. That person does not expect anything at such a moment and therefore he will not be surprised if what he wants does not come true. Still, the likelihood that what he wants does come true, has also become much greater. Banishing every desire, even the desire to receive my blessing, is of the utmost importance to acquire my grace. To ask for something, no matter how well intended, implies desire, doesn't it? And by doing so Man comes in a paradoxical situation. The only correct lesson is that Swami goes along with the desire, and then when it is not fulfilled, confronts Man with himself.

Q: And yet things often do come true the way You said they would.

B: Then the desire for affirmation or for certain things was much less intense. Then there was only a state of being open - of being empty - to accept my guidance, whatever the consequences. When someone communicates with me in that manner, I cannot withstand it and each desire, even a subconscious one, will be realized.

Q: Even when it is not pure?

B: What you ask now is impossible because of the law of inverse logic. If I satisfy a person's desire, this person was pure. It cannot be otherwise.

Q: And yet, don't people sometimes get what they desire, without believing in You or believing in God?. Even very wicked people?

B: Here quite another process is going on. This has to do with Karma. In accordance with the law of Karma it may be predestined for a person to see his desire satisfied. However, that was not the starting point for what you wanted to know.

Q: No, that is true, but I do find it interesting. Could You say more about it? Does that mean that some people have a very blessed life because of their Karma?

B: It may seem blessed, but it isn't. As long as things are given in accordance with Karma, man builds up more Karma and gets more and more entangled in the nets of illusion, of Maya. It could very well take many lives before he has freed himself from those entanglements.

Q: Yes, that I understand. It is indeed quite a different matter. I was talking

71

about people who have turned to You (or God in whatever form) and who see You as their guide and adviser in everything they do.

B: Exactly, and as they become more and more pure and live in accordance with the path of Dharma, of truth, their desires will be less; even the desire for me, and the more strongly I will be present and satisfy their every desire. Because they no longer desire.

Q: You satisfy their every desire, but they have no desires anymore, how can that be?

B: Just as a mother with her child. Even before the child is aware of what it needs or wants, the mother has already taken care of it. When I take the care of a devotee upon myself, he need not desire anything anymore, for everything will be granted to him by me. The only thing that is important is to trust me completely, also when things seem difficult.

Q: Or when they do not go the way he wants them to?

B: There it is again; such a devotee desires nothing anymore. Everything is fine, for I am him, he is me. What could be left to desire? Wherever he finds himself, I am. Whatever he does, I do. Whatever happens to him, happens to me.

Q: Also pain and fear?

B: Also pain and fear. And precisely by not questioning anything, but accepting it, asking for my help without insisting on a solution, accepting what happens as coming from me, precisely then everything will be removed from him and pain and fear will no longer exist. All that is left is a pure trust, "God, do with me what You want, not what I want".

Q: It seems very difficult.

B: It is very simple. It is everything. Everything comes down to that. There is no difference. I am with all of you, each and every minute. Always. However, this person, the one who offers me his total trust, he is the one who has realized me. The one who really knows of my Omnipresence. And no harm will touch him.

Q: As You said before, "To others it may seem that he suffers a lot, but the suffering does not touch him"? (see lesson 14)

B: That is correct.

Q: It seems to me that such complete trust is very hard to acquire.

B: It isn't. Live in accordance with the five human values (truth, righteousness, inner peace, love and non-violence), be happy, see everything as coming from me. Start doing so today in everything you do. That is the way to build character. Offer everything to me and be focused on me at all times. Nothing can go wrong then. Never.

24
GOD-CONSCIOUSNESS

30 July 1994
In India

I am sitting in the hall of the canteen of Baba's ashram in Whitefield waiting for dinner. Even though there are many people going to and fro, I still have the feeling that Baba wants me to write for Him. I ask myself if there are any questions and then I get the inner message, "write about God-consciousness".

Question: Is there something I should know about God-consciousness?

Baba: There is a lot that you and others should know about it.

Q: But I don't have any questions, Baba.

B: God-consciousness is part of the earth-consciousness. It is that part that is the Creator of the earth but that has ended up at a subconscious level of the earth and humanity as well as of the individual human being. Now the time has come for not only the individual but large numbers of people to tap this subconscious level. This is my mission: to make people aware of the God-consciousness which exists in everyone at a subconscious level.

Q: Why has it ended up at that level?

B: This has to do with the era in which we live, the Kali Yuga. Only when God-consciousness has been virtually erased from the conscious living and thinking part of humanity - what they call conscious, that is - will Krishna appear again for the multitudes.

Q: And Krishna is You?

B: I am Krishna who has responded to the distress of many. I have come to save all, to uplift the earth to a conscious level, a God-conscious level.

Q: And this happens individually, each person at a time?

B: No, people have been chosen to help me in this task.

Q: Am I right in thinking (which I did yesterday) that through every person who comes to the ashram and opens up to You, thousands of others are helped?

B: That is partly correct. The numbers may differ. It is true, however, that most people who come here do not only come for themselves.

Q: Baba, I find it hard to understand how You can be at the same time in all those people here and also in all those countless others who are not here.

B: That is precisely God-consciousness. My consciousness slumbers in everyone, like candles that are already there, that are only waiting to be lit by me, by my divine light. I do not give people a new consciousness, I give them themselves, that for which they are on earth, for which they live and exist.

Q: And the people that now recognise you as God are, as it were, the pioneers?

B: There have always been people who recognised God and now also there are people who are conscious of the divine without recognising me, but partly this is true. The people who recognise me as God were born for this. They have taken this birth in order to pass on their radiance to others, once they have recognised me.

Q: Do they do that consciously?

B: Usually it happens unconsciously. It goes beyond the mind. It is even possible that these "messengers" are not loved by the people around them. For what they do is make others conscious of their character faults. They often serve as mirrors for others.

Q: But when others cannot see this, then who benefits by it?

B: The day will come that all my "messengers" will be understood by others. Not directly as messengers, but as pure souls who are not to be blamed for the slander which was poured out over them. People will start recognising themselves, first by realising that they themselves are the ones that make mistakes, then by trying to correct their mistakes and when they have freed themselves to a large extent of their mistakes, they will become God-conscious, conscious of their divine nature.

Q: Are we all part of You, God?

B: You are all God. Your consciousness is as divine as mine, only you don't know it. This ignorance must be removed. But this can only happen if man lives a pure, clean life. Only then is man able to recognize his true nature. My messengers work all over the world as role-models for many. As soon as people have opened up to me, an interaction can take place between me, the messenger and the people who have opened up to me.

Q: But You say that You do not use people as mediums.

B: I don't. I make people God-conscious, so that they, as themselves with their own responsibility, can uplift others to become themselves, in my name.

Actually I find it rather strange that Baba gives me a "lesson" here - a crowded hall, opposite the stairs, a coming and going of people - and what it is that Baba wants to let me know, is not really clear to me.

Q: Are all those people I see here God-conscious?

B: Many are.

Q: But they look exactly like anybody else, that is, mo t of them. To my mind there are only a few that radiate Divinity. They talk, laugh, are busy, quite normal actually.

B: Still, all these people are God-conscious or in the process of becoming so.

Q: So, to look at them there is not much difference between them and others who are not God-conscious?

B: There is, but only a few can see it. A person can only start seeing the divine in others when he has first learned to love himself. And he can only do that, when he has become completely pure, then he will start loving everybody else, because he will experience himself in everybody else.

Q: Is that what You do?

B: Yes, that happens when I look at people.

Q: You are Yourself then?

B: Yes.

Q: How is that possible?

B: It is possible. One cannot really argue about it, but it is the truth. The real truth beyond Maya.

Q: Do you also see Yourself in beggars, murderers and the like?

B: Of course, there is no difference.

Q: But they aren't God-conscious, are they?

B: Their God-consciousness is still deeply hidden, but they are as much God-conscious as those in whom the God-consciousness has come more to the fore.

Q: But don't You condemn their mistakes?

B: Does a mother condemn the mistakes of her child? The only thing she does is correct them, because she knows that the child will be unhappy if it continues making mistakes. That is why I am on earth. To correct you, to transform you, to raise you to your true nature. You are all my children. I love you all as I love myself. We are one.

Q: Is there a difference between God-consciousness and divine consciousness?

B: Someone who has arrived at God-consciousness, who is aware of God-consciousness, such a person has or will get a divine consciousness. That depends on the extent to which he has realised it. The one results from the other, but they are not synonymous. Eventually every cell in the body will become filled with God-consciousness. The person who does not think in terms of "mine" and "yours" anymore has a divine consciousness. He has liberated himself from the bonds of separateness.

Q: So, someone in whom god-consciousness has been lit, is one with You?

B: So is someone in whom that hasn't happened. He is also one with me, only he is less conscious of it. Only when man has a divine consciousness, does he know that there is no difference between him and me. For the time being he will have to accept this as a fact in order to continue on the spiritual path.

25
A BLANK STATE OF BEING

3 August 1994

Baba often looked at me during bhajan-singing, very long and very seriously, but... I only felt blank and that disquieted me.

Question: Baba, You often looked at me, but I couldn't gauge Your look. Nothing seemed to happen, or did it?

Baba: Yes, it did.

Q: But what?

B: I never look at anyone for no reason.

Q: But why don't I know it then?

B: If the time is right, you will know everything; everything you need to know, that is. For the moment that time hasn't come yet.

Q: Baba, actually I feel a little strange. I find it very strange that I felt so blank.

B: That is not strange. Eventually you will go beyond the mind and then you will arrive at a blank state of BEING.

Q: But I don't find that at all nice.

B: It is nice, though. You didn't find it nice, because you were not really blank, there were all kinds of thoughts in your head and you didn't know which to give priority to.

Q: A sort of monkey-mind?

B: Yes, something like that.

Q: But You know that I want to get a God-mind (God-consciousness).

B: Yes, I know.

Q: Then what is it that keeps me from it?

B: You yourself are keeping you from your Self.

Q: Are most people like that?

B: Yes.

Q: Why?

B: They want to be good, but they can't.

Q: What stops them?

B: What stops them is their ignorance about who they are; what stops you is your ignorance about who you are.

Q: I know that I am God.

B: Do you really know?

Q: No, I think that I ought to know, because you told us so.

B: That is the very problem. You don't know it really.

Q: But how will I ever know it really?

B: By not wondering about it anymore, by just BEING, by letting things go the way they go.

Q: As long as things go well, I am able to do that, Baba, but if something threatens to go wrong, I want to take action.

B: Yes, you still have not enough faith in me. I am the one who takes care of things, you do not need to do that.

26
LIFE IS A GAME

7 August 1994

A few days later I am disturbed again, but now because I have the feeling that Baba didn't see me at all during Darshan.

Question: Baba, I feel sad, because You didn't look at me during Darshan.

Baba: Sadness is an attachment that you have to overcome.

Q: Yes, but if I feel it, I feel it.

B: Do you really feel it or do you imagine that you feel it?

Q: I don't know.

B: You do know, but you don't want to admit it to yourself. You know that you are not really sad. It is all a game and you go along with it. But be careful, do not identify yourself with the part you play, that is attachment. As long as you know that you are in a game, you may be sad, if you so choose. But when you are no longer able to distinguish the game from reality, you are stuck, you are then bound to the material world. And that is the very thing that you should prevent from happening. Besides, it is not my form that is with you.

Q: What is with me then?

B: Your own Self. The immortal Atma. What you see in my form is only a faint reflection of it.

Q: But when Your eyes look at us, isn't there a lot that happens, Baba?

B: My eyes also see you without you knowing it. Whether I look at you or not is of no importance. For there is no way that you can gauge my look and the meaning of it. It is "ego" to be so keen about wanting to see. Being seen by God, that is what it is all about. And God sees everything and everyone.

Q: So, if I detach myself from the game, everything is all right?

B: You must play the game, that is why you are here on earth. However, you should not identify yourself with your part. If that is what you mean with "detach yourself", then the answer is "yes". If you mean: to withdraw from your part, then the answer is "no". That is not possible. Courage and patience are the qualities that a Sadhaka should demonstrate. The victory will be great. Show yourself worthy of being such a Sadhaka.

27
DOUBTS

25 August 1994

Since I have returned from India there are several doubts about myself and the "messages" despite the fact that He blessed the manuscript. This, in turn, makes me sad. When I ask Baba for advice, He tells me among other things the following:

Baba: Wavering is necessary to achieve God-consciousness. Doubts also. These are processes to purify the soul, to make it humble, ready for me. "Never have doubts" can only become a reality when you know what doubts are and when you have laboured through them. So, "never have doubts" about your doubts. Let them exist in co-existence with being sure. These two things can exist side by side. Go through it and enjoy it.

Question: Enjoy it?

Baba: Of course, the game of life is a comedy, a drama or a tragi-comedy. Look at it and enjoy the performance. Just know that it is a game, that is all. What does it all matter then, the more dramatic the actor, the more the play draws the attention of the spectator. And at this moment you are both the actor and the spectator. Make sure that the spectator represents your true Self and enjoy the performance of the actor.

28
EVERYTHING IS ATMA

17 October 1994

Question: Baba, there is something I don't understand. I do not know if this is the right moment to ask questions (I am sitting in the garden enjoying the autumn sun), but I would like to try.

Baba: Go ahead.

Q: A few days ago I suddenly realized (with an inner knowledge, not intellectually) that everything is Spirit. Not only man, animal, plant, matter, but also the air around us. We people have, as it were, encapsulated that Spirit in a body, but outside of us it is as much present as inside. So, there is no difference between what is in us and what is outside of us, is that right?

B: Yes.

Q: But then that Spirit would also be in, for instance, a computer?

B: That is correct.

Q: Then what is the difference between a human being and a computer?

B: The difference is that a human being is conscious of the fact that he is Spirit, that he is animated by Spirit, that he exists from Spirit, and a computer is not.

Q: So, if I understand correctly: lifeless matter is not conscious of the Spirit and living matter is.

B: That is correct.

Q: And stones, minerals, plants and animals, are they also conscious of the Spirit?

B: To an evergrowing extent. Consciousness in minerals exists, but is of an entirely different nature than that in people. Their nature is much slower

83

Q: What do You mean by that?

B: Consciousness is a vibration. The consciousness-vibration of minerals is infinitely slower than that of people. The consciousness-vibration of a plant is again much slower than that of an animal and the consciousness-vibration of an animal is again much slower than that of man.

Q: Are there also differences between the different animals?

B: Certainly. Animals also know gradations of consciousness-vibration.

Q: So, it is not the Spirit (or soul) that is different in us and everything else.

B: No, the Spirit is one.

Q: It is consciousness?

B: Yes.

Q: So, what we aim at, as human beings, is the greatest possible extent of consciousness.

B: Yes. One should be conscious of oneself, of the Self that permeates everything.

Q: We are that Self, but is for instance a computer also that Self?

B: In as far as everything is permeated by Spirit - the Atma - a computer is also the Self. A computer, however, will never be conscious of the Self. Lifeless matter can have the task of being useful to man. One could say that it has made itself available, has sacrificed itself to be useful to man.

Q: What about weapons then?

B: The usefulness of many a thing is doubtful, but the sacrifice remains the same. It is man who has the choice to make use of matter in a good or bad way.

Q: Is our body actually also matter which is made use of by the Self?

B: That is a way to look at it.

Q: Still, I have much more control over my body than for instance over that computer, and certainly when it concerns the computer of someone else. And where it concerns someone else's body I have no control at all. If there is no difference, how can that be?

B: As long as consciousness is growing, as long as it has not yet been completed, it will limit itself to that body in which it has been given the opportunity to grow. Once that has happened optimally - and for that, countless

84

lives are needed, from mineral up to enlightened human being—once that has been accomplished, consciousness will then be able to know everything and everyone as well as it knows the body in which it is housed. Besides, when consciousness is still at an initial stage, it is not even able to know its own housing.

Q: Is that why it is so important to first know ourselves?

B: Of course, first know yourself, your lower self, then your higher self, conquer with that higher self the lower self and all will be known.

Q: Is understanding and knowing everything and everyone a criterion then of how far our consciousness has developed?

B: No, it isn't. It is not a step by step process. Only when consciousness has been fully realised, will everything and everyone be known. Suddenly, in a flash. It is not so that when consciousness is growing, the insight into everything and everyone is growing too.

Q: Still, that happens sometimes.

B: People think that it happens. It is a wrong track. As long as one does not know oneself completely, trying to know others is absurd.

Q: What about all those healers, fortune-tellers and psychics then? Are they all realised souls, who know themselves completely?

B: Some of them are; the majority, however, are trapped in illusion. In their case this is of a dual nature. Either they are dangerous and deceitful and the person who comes to them for help will have his hopes shattered in the end, or they are working in a pure way, but to a large extent unconscious. Their work for others is in that case work for their own Self. To the extent that these people dedicate themselves to others with a pure heart, to that extent will others benfit by it. That is my will. I have willed it so. As soon as this person forgets it, his faculty of healing other people will diminish. As long as this person is conscious of that fact and as long as he is also conscious of the fact that by healing others he heals his own Self, his faculty will increase. Until he has arrived at a realised, pure consciousness. Therefore it can be a way to reach me, it can never be a way for the sake of one's own ego. For some time it may seem that such an ego-oriented person is successful in treating people, but that is only my will to completely immerse this person in the ego-entanglement. Only when he realises this, will he be able to rescue himself from it.

Q: Can this be spread out over several lives?

B: That is possible, but it can also take place in one life.

Q: So, in order to realise our consciousness optimally, it is not necessary to be gradually more and more able to heal others.

B: It is of absolutely no importance. If you wish to do it along those lines, that is fine, but with all the dangers that were just pointed out. It is better to keep yourself detached from others, to focus purely on God, on your Self.

Q: But if I live like that, it seems to me as if I do not understand others at all anymore, isn't that bad then?

B: It is bad only when it occupies your mind, when it worries you. Let it go, focus on me.

Q: And when consciousness is complete, I will understand everything and everybody?

B: Yes. However this should not be your motivation, that would keep you again from the goal. Your motivation should be at all times to reach the Self. To reach me.

Q: You are the Self?

B: Yes.

Q: I know, then why is it still so difficult?

B: It is not difficult.

Q: Then why does it take such a long time?

B: Take in mind a stone and take in mind a human being. Can you imagine that it takes time to evolve from one to the other? The time it takes, however, is unimportant. God is time, there is nothing but time.

Q: But You said that time doesn't exist.

B: For the Atma time doesn't exist. For it always IS. For the growth of consciousness God divided Himself in time/space.

Q: And what about matter?

B: Matter is time/space cast into a mould. Without time/space no matter. The one is indissolubly bound up with the other.

Q: So, God is also matter?

B: Of course God is also matter. God is everything. Everything is permeated by God and everything is God.

Q: And what about consciousness?

B: It is that part of God which wanted to be revealed through Creation.

Q: Is the reason for Creation to give form to consciousness?

B: That is correct.

Q: So, what it is all about, is to reach consciousness of the existence of the Spirit. That is why we are on earth and that is why matter is available to us.

B: Yes.

Q: So, it is not all the Spirit that it is all about.

B: No, the Spirit is. Always and everywhere.

Q: You mean, it is there anyway.

B: Yes, whether you are conscious of it or not, is of no importance to the Spirit.

Q: Do You mean by the Spirit the Atma?

B: I mean Paramatma.

Q: What is the difference?

B: Atma is a subdivision of Paramatma.

Q: And Jivatma?

B: Jivatma is the individual Atma in everyone. The Atma which seemingly divided itself.

Q: Are all Jivatmas together Paramatma?

B: Yes, but every Jivatma is in itself also Paramatma.

Q: As soon as it is conscious of that fact?

B: No, always.

Q: Then what's the difference?

B: As soon as man has reached the consciousness to know that, suffering will have disappeared.

Q: Is that the reason why we must let our consciousness grow?

B: It is the other way around. Because of the fact that suffering exists, we want to escape from it and that can only be done by being conscious of our divine nature, in which there is no suffering. Suffering, as it were, acts as a sting to make our consciousness optimal.

Q: To escape from suffering is not the ultimate goal, but the incentive to reach the ultimate goal, is that what You mean?

B: Yes.

Q: When a body has died, it is still matter; does it still have a soul then?

B: Yes.

Q: But doesn't the soul leave the body when we die?

B: Consciousness leaves the body when we die, consciousness separates itself from the soul, does not form a unity anymore with the soul.

Q: Baba, I don't understand. Doesn't the body disintegrate completely. What happens to the soul then?

B: The Spirit or soul IS, without or with a body. The encapsulation of the Spirit dissolves, that is all.

Q: And the individual soul, the Jivatma?

B: It dissolves again into the Paramatma, into all and everyone, into existence.

Q: So, it is accumulated consciousness that leaves the body. And the extent of it differs from person to person?

B: That is partly correct. The soul was, is and will ever be, it never leaves a body and it is never born in a body. Consciousness of the Atma creates a body in which the animated matter can make that consciousness grow.

Q: But I have heard that it is the Atma that creates a body.

B: The consciousness of the Atma is at the same time the soul, since everything is Atma. There is nothing that is non-Atma.

Q: So, ultimately realised consciousness is Atma?

B: Yes.

Q: I think that I am starting to understand it: that is why time doesn't actually exist. We need time because matter is time/space and we need time/space to obtain consciousness of the immortal soul, the Atma. And when that consciouness has been completely and optimally obtained, it will appear that that consciousness had been the soul - the Atma - all along and that time did not exist at all.

B: Put into words you come close. However, it cannot be put into words, because words also are subject to time/space which doesn't exist.

Q: Then what about the primordial sound "OM"?

B: "OM" is one and indivisible. From "OM" everything originated.

Q: Is "OM" the same as Paramatma?

B: Yes.

29
PERFECTION

19 October 1994

I have been rather tired lately and I have the feeling that I haven't come to anything. When I ask Baba for the reason, He lets me know that an inner spiritual transformation is always accompanied by a loss of energy.

Question: Is it a kind of in-between stage in which I am now?

Baba: Yes.

Q: But why does that take energy?

B: It is as if you are trying to open a door that does not really yield. A thick, heavy door. As long as the door has not been oiled well and does not yield, pushing it open takes energy.

Q: For whom am I opening a door?

B: For me, to let me in.

Q: But that is what I really want. Why doesn't that door just open then?

B: Because there is still too much resistance. The hinges jam, as it were.

Q: How will they become flexible then?

B: By not worrying about anything. By accepting things the way they are.

Q: Will I be less tired then?

B: No, that tiredness belongs to it. If you should have lots of energy, you would not be able to stay calm and let things be what they are.

Q: But why is rest so important?

B: There is an inner process going on, in which you try to find your way. You sense things correctly, but you can't give it a name and that worries you. Don't give it a name. Eventually there is only one name.

Q: That of God?

B: Yes.

Q: So, I ought to name everything God.

B: Yes.

Q: Is that the oil that will make the door flexible?

B: Yes.

Q: Is there more, Baba?

B: There is more.

Q: But I don't have any more questions.

B: For what you need to know, no questions are needed. You should know that I am always with all of you. That there is only one life, the divine existence. In it is no separateness. There is only pure BEING and that pure BEING is what must be reached.

Q: But how?

B: By being pure; not doing anything, being quiet, listening.

Q: Baba, I am listening, but I don't hear anything. I do feel very peaceful, though. The room is so beautiful; the light is beautiful, the pets are inside and sleep quietly. All is well and calm. Is that it?

B: Yes.

Q: But in a short while everything will be different, and tomorrow things will be different again. Everything changes constantly, where is the unity then?

B: It is within.

Q: Within everything?

B: Yes.

Q: Then why don't I see it? With my intelligence I might be able to reason about that unity, but I cannot see it, none of us "normal" people can.

B: What you see is all one. What you see is God in His innumerable diversity of forms.

Q: That everything together forms God, I am able to understand, but that is quite something else than that everything in itself is God, isn't it?

B: Together every part forms the whole, but each part in itself is also the whole.

Q: That I don't understand, Baba. I don't find our world that perfect.

B: Seen from the Atma only perfection exists.

Q: All right, Baba, I look at my dog now, for example. She is indeed perfect. Everything works together in such a way that she walks, looks, eats, barks, is interested, sits down, sleeps, etc. That is real perfection.

B: In the same way everything is perfect when you look at it and observe it.

Q: And that is unity?

B: Yes.

Q: But suppose that the same dog is ill?

B: Then perfection lies in the combined action of illness and body.

Q: But surely perfection isn't the same as unity?

B: Why not?

Q: Because, for instance, my dog is not my cat. They are two separate animals.

B: Both are perfect, though?

Q: Yes, I cannot deny that.

B: They could not be anything else than who they are, can they?

Q: No, they are who they are.

B: That makes them one and unique.

Q: I am starting to understand it a little, but then that is a different kind of unity than that everything is one.

B: Unity is not synonymous with similarity. Unity is a state of perfection which is evergrowing. Your dog is one. Your cat is one. The room in which the dog and cat are, is one. The house in which the room is, is one. The city in which the house is, is one and so on.

Q: Yes, but my house, for instance, is not perfect.

B: It exists, doesn't it?

Q: Yes.

B: Then it is perfect.

Q: But if, for instance, the roof would leak?

B: Then it would be a perfect house with a leaking roof.

Q: But something that leaks can't be perfect, can it?

B: Why not? Perfection consists of things, people, animals being as they are, with their shortcomings. They exist, therefore they are perfect. They ARE. BEING is perfection. There is nothing else. It is about the essence, the state of BEING.

Q: And that is God?

B: Yes, it is God, revealed in time. Perfection is a state of being, which changes from second to second.

Q: And that is unity?

B: Yes, compare it to a kaleidoscope. The kaleidoscope is the whole. Each fragment is perfect and unique. The combinations are many, but within a certain definition and limit.

Q: But I don't understand the "why" of it all, Baba.

B: There is no "why". Only a "Be Cause", as you have been told before (see chapter 19). Don't ask yourself anything. Face it. Accept. Enjoy. Experience. BE.

Q: At this moment I can sense in some way what it is, just being, because I am sitting so quietly here, but when I have to do all sorts of things it is not that simple.

B: Go beyond the thoughts, don't ask yourself anything. Establish yourself in BEING. Become familiar with the kaleidoscopic concept of unity.

30
COMMUNICATION

18 November 1994

I am sad about someone and I would like to talk about it with that person. Baba lets me know that that is not necessary, that I should be detached. That I can communinicate with Him.

Question: But can I communicate with You in the same way as I do with other people?

Baba: Of course.

Q: But with You I often don't know if it is my longing that makes You say something, or that it is really You.

B: With other people you don't know that either.

Q: That I don't understand.

B: Every human contact is a reflection of the soul-state of the other. There is no other in fact. It is all one and indivisible. What you hear the other say about you, says as much about the other. And what the other says about himself, says as much about you.

Q: But isn't that very awkward?

B: It can be awkward; most of the time it isn't, because people have taken that into consideration in their contact with others.

Q: Are they aware of it?

B: Most people aren't. It is the same as with looking at things: what we see is crossed in our brains, so that we still see things the way they present themselves to us. The same holds good for mutual communication. Our hearing makes us hear things in such a way that what we hear is attuned to our reception-channel. In other words, we hear what suits us to hear.

Q: But we can be enormously insulted or abused. We didn't want to hear that, did we?

B: If you feel insulted by it, it means that you wanted to hear it. Otherwise you would be able to reflect it back to the other, as it always reveals something of the other and usually not of the person at whom it was aimed.

Q: Doesn't that make life complicated?

B: Life is a game. Participate in it. But know that the game can be played at different levels. Choose yourself at which level you want to participate in it. If you let yourself be overpowered by someone else with sorrow or words, it is your choice as well.

31
THE POPE

25 December 1994

It is Christmas day and I just saw the Pope on television. He touched me in a special way and I knew that Baba had something to do with it. For me this was something totally unexpected; I never think of the Pope and I have absolutely no opinion of him, good or bad. When I ask Baba about it, He gives me among other things the following "lesson":

Question: Is the Pope a spiritually superior person?

Baba: Yes.

Q: But He doesn't want to have anything to do with You?

B: He doesn't need to, he is open to God, to Jesus. Jesus is the form of God that he professes. The Pope is a pure, almost realised soul.

Q: Were all Popes?

B: No.

Q: Do You work through the Pope?

B: Yes.

Q: Is he aware of it?

B: He is aware of the fact that he is an instrument of God, that is sufficient.

Q: Can he change the world?

B: No.

Q: Why not?

B: His strength lies in passing on, in continuing what was. Not in renewing. What comes is transformation.

97

Q: So, he is not able to transform people?

B: No.

Q: Are there people who are?

B: There are.

Q: People like Jesus, Ramakrishna, Francis of Assisi and the like?

B: Yes, saints and sages.

Q: And gurus?

B: Some, not all.

Q: And if the Pope should be completely realised?

B: Then he will die. He is not on earth to transform. He is on earth to perpetuate.

Q: But why, that is hardly of any use to anyone anymore, is it?

B: Yes it is; for many people he is an anchorage in these times.

Q: Baba, what the Pope says about birth-control, that surely can't be right?

B: It can, what the Pope does is my will. Man himself is responsible for his deeds. The Pope indicates what is God's will.

Q: But man does something different from what You want.

B: Man also does what I want, only not in the manner that I want it.

Q: How do You want it?

B: One can practise birth-control by living a celibate life. That is God's will for the people. The Pope doesn't have any choice but to propagate that.

Q: But what about the people who use the pill?

B: As long as man is still trapped in his animal nature, is not able to practise celibacy, it is all right to use birth-control. It is even essential. It is my will for the person that does not live according to God's will.

Q: That way he does live according to Your will.

B: Yes, at an unconscious level, however.

Q: Will the Pope start recognising You?

B: This Pope won't.

Q: And the next?

B: Yes, very soon even.

Q: Do you mean that he will come very soon?

B: No, I mean that he will recognize me soon after he has taken office.

Q: Will he make that publicly known?

B: Not right away. That should happen with caution. The Pope will have to be very prudent. Counter-forces will start to act.

Q: Baba, I don't have any more questions, is there more to come?

B: Yes. You should know that the Catholic Church is one of my pillars. One of the pillars on which I build, on which my Church of the faithful has been established. That Church is timeless, eternal and will always exist. There will always be people who have chosen the form of Jesus as their chosen Deity. Jesus is my Son, whom I love unto eternity. As long as there are people, He will be there.

Q: He is the Saviour for all humanity?

B: For all those who have chosen His form, His essence, as an object of adoration. He (Jesus) assists me in my task on earth.

Q: Are there also others?

B: There are many.

Q: Also unknown people?

B: Yes.

Q: Swami, is there more?

B: There is nothing anymore.

32
MAYA

26 December 1994

I am wondering why some days Baba is much more clearly present in my heart than others. This often does not seem to be related to the things I am doing at that moment at all. On the contrary, when I am involved in Seva (selfless service), I am often not as much aware of Him as when I am just sitting, doing nothing. I have the idea that it has something to do with an inner process, which must progress slowly.

Question: Is that true, Baba?

Baba: It is partly true. The process does not progress slowly at all when you compare it to the many lives you have lived. It is true, though, that you sometimes have to mark time. Man must get used to having me with him, slowly but surely, a little more each time. This cannot be borne all at once. The law of gradualness, and I mean gradualness only in relation to this life, is necessary.

Q: For everyone?

B: For most. After each step forward you are given a respite.

Baba then explains that receptivity to Him is related to the kind of work one performs. When you are very concentrated and accurately doing something, He is present (He always is), but you will not, or hardly, be aware of it.

Q: Is it possible to be aware of it, even during that kind of work?

B: It is possible, but it is not desirable. It distracts. Matter slows down and time accelerates when you are focused on me. Such a situation is not conducive to accurate work.

Q: It bothers me that I don't think of You constantly.

B: It is my grace that makes you think of me. Don't worry, if it does not happen, it is my will. There is nothing you bring about, everything is accomplished by me. What you can do in full awareness is live according to my laws. By living such a life - by putting into practice the 5 human values - you will please me, and you will automatically, when it is my will, think of me. I respond, as it were, to your way of life by my Presence.

Q: Which I don't always feel, is that right?

B: When it keeps you from your work - my work, that is, for everything is my work - you won't feel it.

Q: It all seems so simple and it is so wonderful to live with You and for You, why don't many more people make that relatively simple decision to live a good life?

B: More and more people will make that decision. The law of acceleration has already come into operation. The advance cannot be stopped anymore.

Q: Can living according to the human values be compared with taking the first step toward You, to which You respond with 10 steps toward man?

B: That is correct.

Q: Can everyone do it or do you have to be predestined according to your Karma?

B: Everyone can do it, at all times. Winning God's grace is the name of the game. That is why man lives. As long as he does not do it, he will suffer. In that respect he is free. He has the freedom to live according to Gods commandments now or later. The consequences, however, are also his.

Q: Did You contrive all of that in the beginning?

B: You cannot speak in those terms. There is an eternal existence, an eternal now, in which all develops as it is preordained.

Q: Preordained by You?

B: Yes by me, and in it people have free will to be participants or adversaries.

Q: But why?

B: There is no why, you know that. It is as it is. The plan is still unfolding.

101

God IS. Man BECOMES. When man IS, he is God. Equal to God. One with God. Then there are no questions anymore.

Q: Then I will understand everything?

B: No, that won't be necessary then. Then there is understanding as part of BEING, without the desire to understand. Acceptance, even of incomprehension, has to do with it.

Q: You are God. God created the world, but You say that You did not contrive it?

B: Did a seed contrive the tree? The one developed from the other and IS there simultaneously.

Q: But surely not in the same time?

B: Not in the time that is linked to matter; but it is in the time that is linked to God. God is time. Matter is time. God and matter are two things at the moment. That is the essence of duality. When God and matter have become one through the dissolution of the veil of Maya, time will not exist anymore, there will be a continuous existence then.

Q: But the body will still grow older.

B: The body is like a garment that wears out and must be replaced. In the unity of God and matter things are different.

Q: How are they different then?

B: Present, past and future will then be one. The one is there and the other as well. There are no boundaries, no restrictions anymore. The body, the world, goes through the various stages in the same time - in the ONE time. That is unity.

Q: Does it have to do with a dimension that we do not know?

B: It has to do with 36 dimensions that you do not know. Growing old is something like pronouncing a sentence. It seems to happen in time, but it is a statement of one and the same which is indivisible.

Q: But even pronouncing a sentence takes time.

B: Here on earth it certainly does, as duality reigns here and God and matter are separate.

Q: So, my body is young, middle-aged and old in one and the same moment, and not only this body, but that of all previous and future lives as well?

B: That is a way to understand it.

Q: Can it be really understood by us?

B: No it can't, because there is nothing else but time in which you can think. Thinking itself requires time at the level of attainment of humanity.

Q: So, something timeless cannot be contrived?

B: Knowledge presents itself in a flash.

Q: And that flash cannot be translated into words, because that would take time again?

B: That is how it is.

Q: So, actually one should not talk about it?

B: One cannot talk about it.

Q: So, the Atma is eternal and avails itself of a body?

B: That is the way to understand and express it in earthly terms.

Q: But when Atma and body have become one, the body will still grow old.

B: The body does not exist at all. There is no birth, no death, it is all appearance, illusion, the game of Maya. Atma IS, there is nothing else.

Q: But I want to have a better understanding of it.

B: Compare it to a dream. In a dream you can experience all sorts of things and you can be everywhere. You are, however, at one place and hardly any time passes.

Q: Yes, I see. So, life is as a dream?

B: Yes. This life on earth, the past, the future, it is all a dream.

Q: And the present?

B: The present is the point where the dream is dreamed. It is, in fact, the only mainstay. Should the present fall away, illusion would stop existing.

Q: So, the present is Maya?

B: That is correct.

33
INCLUSIVENESS

22 January 1995

There is a problem which I don't seem to be able to solve. On the one hand I would like very much what happens between Baba and me to be exclusive - an exclusive love - and at the same time I know with my intelligence that that is nonsense. What's more, if that were so, that very exclusiveness would be based on nothing. If others should not receive as much love from Him as I do, that love of His would not be of very great significance, and still... at the same time I would very much like to have an exclusive bond with Baba.

Question: Baba, will You help me with this?

Baba: Yes.

Q: Please explain it to me.

B: My contact with each of you is exclusive, is unique and is especially attuned to the one for whom it is meant.

Q: So, when I feel that I have an exclusive bond with You, it is true?

B: Yes, it is absolutely true.

Q: And everyone could believe that of himself.

B: Every one of you should know that and experience it, that's what it is all about.

Q: But it is so difficult, I think, because here on earth exclusiveness implies that nobody else is involved.

B: Here we have again the problem of earthly consciousness. Only God can maintain such a contact with each of you that there still can be talk of exclusiveness. When you start understanding this with your entire being, when you start realising this in the true sense of the word, in other words: make it real, then you will have solved the dilemma in which you find yourself.

Q: Is exclusiveness really the right word then?

B: Let's put it this way: your contact with God is exclusive to the extent that no other contact of mine with anyone else goes along the same lines. It is not exclusive, if you understand by it that no other human being, except you, has contact with God. Seen from God there is no exclusive contact with anyone, for humanity is one. God has divided himself in many parts that have established themselves in man as Atma, from which contact is maintained. Exclusive means excluding everything else. God works, as it were, inclusive, meaning: including everyone and everything else. That inclusiveness is an all-embracing existence, an all-embracing knowledge and an all-embracing plan.

Q: How do You mean that?

B: God's plan is at the same time its execution. There is no plan which results in execution; it is all-embracing, which means, "it is all in one." An inclusive plan as it were.

Q: But if, for instance, we make things, build houses, construct throughways, establish schools etc., then those things weren't there first and later on they were.

B: In the earthly dimension it is like that. In God it is totally different. It was there first, it is there now and it will always be there. It is all stored away in the plan that is all-embracing.

Q: But how can I understand that, Baba? Could You give an example of it, which is comprehensible to me?

B: Imagine that you are travelling by train from town A to town B. Both town A and town B exist already and the train by which you travel also exists already. For you it takes time and it requires a plan to go from A to B, but seen objectively from A or from B or from the train, that time doesn't exist. They exist already, don't they?

Q: It becomes a little clearer now. If time didn't exist, I would be simultaneously in A and in B?

B: You *are* simultaneously in A and in B, but because of the limitation of time and space you do not experience it as such.

Q: But You said that God is time and You said that God is space.

B: Time and space also form part of the all-embracing plan. Time and space form part of God's inclusiveness.

Q: So, what feels to me as an exclusive contact with You, is in reality an inclusive contact?

B: From your point of view it is exclusive, your path with me is yours and no one follows the same path. From my point of view it is inclusive. Precisely because it is inclusive, you experience it as exclusive. Know that each of you has an exclusive contact with me. Not one creature on earth, from the smallest up to the highest, can escape my inclusiveness. Do not feel burdened by it anymore, when you have the feeling that you maintain an exclusive bond with me, but don't attach any feelings of superiority to it either. Be One without a second and know that each of you is One without a second.

Q: Do all of us together, each as a part, form the unity, or is each one of us in itself that unity?

B: Both.

Q: How can that be?

B: Again, is your starting-point exclusiveness or is it inclusiveness. On earth, as said before, it seems as if everything consists of either one or the other. But what it is all about is: one as well as the other. Both are true. You on earth form together One and each of you is in itself One; and this expands more and more, for the earth is in itself One, but also forms part of and therefore is the whole cosmos.

Q: So, then man is also the whole cosmos?

B: That is correct.

Q: But I can't understand that.

B: No, it is never to be understood intellectually. Once all of you will experience it.

Q: When?

B: When the time for it has come.

Q: You already said that that will not be for everyone at the same time.

B: That is true, that also belongs to the all-embracing, inclusive plan.

Q: So, God's plan is still unfolding?

B: Yes and no. Yes, if you think in terms of time/space; no, if you think from God's inclusiveness. Everything exists already.

Q: In the sense that You, for instance, know now already how old I will become, or when a building will be demolished and what will come in its place?

B: I know that indeed, but that in itself is only a part, which still takes place in time/space. Everything exists already without beginning or end. There is no beginning and there is no end. There is only "this" for all eternity.

Q: And "this" is filled with happiness?

B: "This", the present, is happiness, is love, is oneness, is everything.

Q: And You have come on earth to make us experience it?

B: Eventually that is the goal, to submerge you in the bliss from which you all have originated.

Q: Then what about all those wars?

B: They do not exist in the inclusiveness. They only exist in the exclusiveness. And as such they have a function, just like disasters and diseases.

Q: But isn't that awful?

B: Awful is: to let it pass without finding it awful.

Q: Who do You mean, the one who goes through those ordeals or the others?

B: Both. Suffering is also a way of contact with God. Exclusive contact for the one who undergoes it and for the one who has something to do with it, inclusive where it concerns God.

Q: All right, Baba, suppose town A is happiness, town B is suffering and the train is me. I understand that all of it exists at the same time, but why would I sit down in that train to go to B?

B: You don't go to B. A and B are one, there is no difference.

Q: Well, that's difficult.

B: Once again, it is not to be understood by the intellect and what you try to do is express in words what cannot be understood by the intellect, therefore it can't be understood by words.

Q: Is it better not to try?

B: On the contrary; it is good because an answer is possible all the same, despite its elusiveness. This is the answer that penetrates the deeper layers of your consciousness, beyond the intellect, beyond the mind. That part in you and in others that knows what it is all about and that can so develop into becoming more and more receptive to divine knowledge.

34
ACCEPTANCE

11 March 1995

For a few days I have been rather sad because one of my cats is seriously ill. There is a great chance that she will die. In one of His "lessons" Baba sets my mind at ease; He takes away many doubts, also about the fact that I feel guilty for being sad and therefore not equal-minded, as He wants us to be.

Question: Baba, when I am worried like this, I am not very equal-minded.

Baba: But you are. It is true that you are overpowered by emotions, but at the same time you are able to perceive them.

Q: Is that equanimity?

B: Yes.

Q: So, it doesn't mean that you never feel emotions anymore?

B: No, it means that you look at yourself and at what happens to you from the point of view of an observer. And when you are overpowered by sadness, then that is what you look at. It is about acceptance of the things that happen, also of the sadness that you experience. Is that what you want to reach, acceptance?

Q: Very much so.

B: Then regard this as a lesson.

Q: So, the lesson lies not in the fact that I ought to accept with equanimity that my cat is very ill, but that I should accept that it hurts that she is ill.

B: Yes. Always focus on me and remember: everything is my will, nothing and no one will pass away before its time.

EPILOGUE to PART 1

In the period of 1970-1973 I wrote about 500 poems in three languages, Dutch, English and French. In most of these poems the longing for merging is clearly present, the merging of all of us with that for which we are destined.

At that time it was something vague for me, something elusive. I often defined that "something", for which I longed, as "You". "You" stood for God, for my soul. "You" was my immortal lover; was the other, for whom I craved. Exactly what it was, I did not know. I was conscious of the fact that it existed both outside of me and within me. Although it was intangible, it provided some sort of deep happiness, often mixed with the pain of melancholy.

I didn't know of Sai Baba. It would take 9 years before I first heard of Him, and another 9 years before I would go to Him for the first time.

Now, looking back on that episode, I can see how almost all of the poems I wrote such a long time ago are about Him, Sai Baba, the Lord of my soul, "You".

Here is one of the poems, which I think clearly illustrates what I mean:

"To become one with You,
And never to withdraw
Within my loneliness.
To be within myself
As if I were with You.
To always go on, knowing
That You are there
And talking to You;
And then to go on
To help this endless game
Of hunger and of sickness,
Of poverty and pain".

Never could I have imagined that one day this would come true so literally, sentence after sentence! And for that I have to thank You, Swami, my Divine master. Sai Baba, who already knew me long before I had any knowledge of Him, and who had then already let me know which path He would walk with me.

OM SAI RAM

111

"You see diversity in what in truth is unity. It is Maya (illusion) which causes this delusory experience of seeing diversity when there is only unity. It is the direct experience of many great sages as given in the Upanishads, that there is only the one unity to be found within all the multiplicity of the world. This unity is the basis for everything everywhere; it is the Atma, which has to be experienced in every object and in every being."

-Sathya Sai Baba

PART 2
God Is One

35
YEARNING AFTER GOD

*

19 July 1995
In India, in Baba's ashram in Puttaparthi

For some days I have been with Baba again. I find quite a lot of things rather confusing and I don't know exactly how to lay out a course. He is often with me in my heart and despite the confusion I experience, I feel peaceful and quiet. But even so, it bothers me that He pays so little attention to me; a few glimpses from afar now and then, of which I am not even sure if they are meant for me, that is all. At the same time I understand why this is happening, it is of course very conducive to the process of reducing my ego.

Question: Dear Baba, please help me to understand what my path is exactly and let me know if I am doing all right. Please grant me inner guidance. You know that I am obedient. If it is clear to me what You want, I will always do what You say. Why do You keep me in such uncertainty about what You intend for me?

Baba: Because you can do it yourself.

Q: But I don't want to be able to do it myself. It must be so wonderful to have You guide me completely. I am getting so tired of having to be able to do and to decide everything myself.

B: I always help you.

Q: But it all stays so vague, unclear, and so does the interaction between me and others.

B: Just continue. Do not expect a revelation in a few days. Life is for that. Continue on your path.

Q: Are there other things, Baba?

B: Many more things.

Q: What are they?

B: Know that I am God, omnipotent, omnipresent, omniscient, seeing everything. Then all the diversity will dissapear.

Q: I know, but I don't understand. How can I arrive at a state of BEING where I don't want to understand anymore?

B: Jnana (knowledge) is BEING. You long for Jnana. Be kind, quiet. Accept what comes. Do not try to get a good place during Darshan at the expense of someone else. Grant another what you would grant yourself.

Q: But that is very difficult Baba, to be so detached as not to care anymore where I will end up sitting. I would like to be able to do that, but often I do not succeed.

B: Patience. A patient has patience. The illness of Maya makes patients of people, students in patience. Things need not be precipitated.

Q: No, just being here is wonderful by itself. Why would or should I want more?

B: You want more because you yearn after the Form.

Q: But didn't the Gopis do the same?

B: Yearning is the way; yearning is devotion. The yearning must grow.

Q: And what about those others (those who do have Your Form)?

B: They must follow their own path.

Q: Yearning does indeed feel sweet. But at the same time wistful.

B: That yearning must completely flow through you. No other thought should exist anymore without yearning after God.

Q: For Your good marks?

B: For my "God-marks".

Q: Is that the same?

B: Yes and no. If you ARE, you ARE and all you do is good. You must yearn and know that God knows and sees everything; that God assesses everything. This must permeate you during every deed, every act you undertake. God assesses, for God you do it. God sees it. God is always with you.

Q: Is that yearning?

B: That is the fulfilment of yearning. That is the empathy of the sweet pain of wistfulness. The soul yearns after itself, after unity. The person in whom the soul-force grows - or rather in whom it manifests more clearly - will experience this yearning. You have to go through it. It is a step on the way to BEING.

Q: Does it have to do with detachment?

B: Of course, by being detached you experience yearning, by being detached yearning becomes a state of BEING and no longer an intellectual game. Long for me with heart and soul. Go through the pain of that longing. If that longing would be assuaged at this moment, it wouldn't be good for you. You would end up in complacency.

Q: And if I promise I won't?

B: You cannot promise that, because for that you don't know yourself well enough.

Q: Is that a character-flaw?

B: It is a "Man-flaw". Man doesn't know his Self anymore. That is the original sin. That is the separation which has taken place between man and God.

Q: God and Self are synonymous?

B: Yes, whoever knows his Self, knows God. Whoever knows God, knows his Self.

Q: Is that Jnana?

B: Yes, that is the knowledge it is all about. The God-knowledge.

Q: Baba, teach me to know myself.

B: Then go through the yearning.

Q: Yes, but I am so selfish. I want You for myself.

B: Every man should want God for himself. There is nothing wrong with that. Just don't be unscrupulous. Respect the other. Realize that there is no difference between his yearning and yours. Realize that unity lies behind that, in the longing to reach God.

Q: Is there more, Baba?

B: Yes, much more.

Q: Right now You are in the interview-room, giving an interview, and I am here corresponding with you, how is that possible?

B: It is possible, this is the proof of it. God is everywhere and sees everything. No one can escape His knowing and seeing all. So, why shouldn't it be possible? Love all people. They want the same as you. Stand up for yourself where it concerns God and respect that another does the same.

Q: Why do some people get an interview and others don't?

B: Why not? Humanity is one. The Self gets an interview. Your Self.

Q: Even so, it makes quite a difference to me whether I or a total stranger sit in the interview room.

B: That is the limitation of separation.

Q: Yes, but at the moment that is reality.

B: Hence the yearning, which will bring your soul home, so that there will be no separation anymore. Be detached. Look at things as if you are free from them. Look at yourself the way you look at others, then every sense of separation falls away, doesn't it?

Q: Yes, then I am just one out of many.

B: Not just, and not one out of many. Than you are one with them and with me.

Q: It seems like a puzzle, in which everyone fits and does his work, is that so?

B: No, God does not make puzzles. God IS. Creation IS. Man in it is part of God. Working is God. Thinking is God.

Q: Writing this is also God?

B: Yes, of course. You write, God writes in you, you write in God.

Q: And the labourers who are working on the roof right now?

B: They also work in God and God works in them.

The interview in the interview room has ended and Baba comes outside. For some time He talks with the men on the porch and while doing so He often looks in the direction of the section in which I am sitting amongst many others. It is too far away to see if He is in fact also looking at me. This goes on for a long time and He looks again and again. All right, Baba, I think, if

You are also looking at me, please let me know this by swaying back and forth, when looking in this direction (the way He sometimes does: He sways slowly back and forth while standing in one place - during the six times that I have been in His Ashram, I have only seen Him do it a few times and I always found it a delightful sight, something not of this world). This is the first time I ask for something like a sign from Him and I am a little ashamed of it, but it came straight from my heart, this inner request.

Baba is still occupied with the men on the porch, busily gesticulating and again and again He looks prolongedly in the direction where I am also sitting. Then He turns to go inside the temple. Just before He enters the temple, He turns around once more, looks again in my direction and starts swaying back and forth for a long time!

36

THE ONLY LEGITIMATE LONGING

20 July 1996

While waiting for morning-Darshan, I think over the lesson of the previous day and I realize that there still is something which is not quite clear to me. Baba teaches us that we must let go of every longing, but what about yearning then?

Question: Is yearning something else than longing?

Baba: Yes.

Q: How then?

B: Longing has to do with another. Yearning is the longing of the soul for its Maker. Yearning has to do with God.

Q: But still, it is some kind of longing, isn't it?

B: It is the only legitimate longing.

Q: I long for You, yearn after You, after real communication with You, after hearing You, after submitting myself to your gaze. Is that yearning or longing?

B: If there is no ego involved, it is yearning. If it is accompanied by ego, by wanting to be seen by others, by wanting others to see that you are receiving attention from me, it is longing and therefore not to be condoned.

37

ILLNESS

5 August 1996

While waiting for Baba to come out, a woman spoke to me about her son who had fallen ill. She told me that she didn't mind, because of the fact that illnesses in the ashram are necessary. "One cannot only be cleansed spiritually and leave the body impure," she said. "That is what we do in the western world. Therefore we get illnesses and become stiff when we get old. Sai Baba gives the people here a very rapid cleansing of the body, so that body and soul will be in tune again. That is why here in the ashram people so often suffer from small wounds, infections, stomach cramps, heavy perspiration etc."

Question: Is this true, Baba?

Baba: Yes.

Q: Can You say more about it?

B: Yes, the body is like a power station which generates energy by combustion. The fuel is a combination of Atma and earthly substance - the material world, as it were. Now, the combustion can only be pure when the earthly substance is pure, because Atma is pure.

Q: I don't understand one iota of it, how can Atma be combustible?

B: Atma is fire *and* what undergoes combustion *and* what alights the fire. Atma is everything, there is only Atma. When the body becomes aware that it is Atma and nothing but Atma, every cell will become God-conscious - or Atma-conscious - and the fuel for the body will be Divine. The combustion-process, the fuel and the ignition will be one then and the body will remain supple. If the body is not conscious of the Atmic principle, but the mind is, there is an imbalance and combustion cannot take place optimally. Remains of unburned matter will stay behind in the body and will accumulate there as toxins which will slowly but surely destroy the body. To the extent that the body gets weaker, its possibility of becoming Atma-conscious to the depth of the cells decreases. My task here is aimed at making the body fit again for the spiritual process and to remove the imbalance that has arisen, by banishing the toxins.

Q: But what about wounds then, and what was the matter with H.? For some time it seemed that she was totally paralysed.

B: They are all shock-therapies for the central nerve system. This has to happen drastically and as a series of shocks, because time is lacking to treat it slowly. When the central nerve system starts identifying itself with the Atma, the body will follow.

Q: And then we will not fall ill anymore?

B: Eventually that no longer need happen, although illness has also to do with supranatural laws.

Q: What do You mean by that?

B: An illness can be something suffered for another person.

Q: But then that other person wouldn't get the shock-effect that is needed, would he?

B: Not every illness has this purpose. Illness can also have a Karmic implication. A debt, as it were, which still has to be settled, whereas the balance is already there.

Q: And one can also take that upon oneself for somebody else?

B: That happens, but one should be careful with it, because the danger of new Karmic involvements becomes greater then.

Q: Therefore, as I understand it now, the reason for illness can be 1) A Karmic working-out of a debt. 2) A shock-effect to bring body and soul into balance. Is there still another reason?

B: There are many other reasons.

Q: Which?

B: An illness is a symptom of the mental state of a person. The illness shows a person his spiritual development. These are, as it were, symptomatic illnesses

Q: Do You mean mental illnesses?

B: Not necessarily, although they do fall within that category. Not every mental illness, however, is symptomatic for the state of the mind. It can also be an indication of the imbalance in the combustion-process.

Q: But then again, if we do not fall ill anymore, we will not die anymore either

122

B: The body is bound to death, but death could take possession of the body in a much more gentle way than is happening at present. The body is subject to wear and tear due to old age, but this need not be accompanied by severe suffering. Eventually death is a state of transition and a balanced person will himself be able to direct this transition along certain lines.

Q: You mean that he will know himself when he is ready to die?

B: Yes, this can happen consciously in a body in which there is no imbalance between Atma and matter.

Q: Baba, it seems to me that illnesses proceed much faster here in the ashram than back at home.

B: Yes, that is usually the case, recovery leading to the state of unity of body and soul is often vehement, but short.

Q: And after such a process of illness, is the body perfect then?

B: No, then the state of the body has been adjusted to the state of development of the consciousness. Subsequently most people who return to their western abodes will again grow faster spiritually than physically, and a physical cleansing will again be necessary.

Q: But don't we also grow spiritually here in the Ashram?

B: Certainly; however, that could happen much more thoroughly, if this physical adjustment was not needed.

Q: Can we also do something about it back home?

B: Yes: Live in a true, pure and simple fashion. Listen to the language of the body. Don't look for comfort. Be disciplined. Live in a regular way. Do not make any distinction between week-days and weekends. Meditate at regular hours, though not too long.

Q: Are there general rules for this?

B: Yes, to be found in Dhyana Vahini.

38
NOT WANTING ANYTHING ANYMORE

6 August 1995
After the last Darshan before leaving for Holland

Baba: You know, don't you, that God sees everything and everyone? Know that God is always with you, wherever you are and that He always sees you.

Question: But I would so much like it to be in the Form.

B: You think that is what you want. You are Atma and Atma doesn't want anything. Do not want anything and you will realize Atma.

Q: But what You ask of me is very difficult.

B: It is the greatest task given to man. Not wanting anything anymore, that's what it is all about.

Q: Is that what You are teaching me?

B: Yes.

Q: Still, when I am here, I would like to sit as close to You as possible, is that wrong?

B: That is what everyone wants. If another sits close to me, then you are sitting close to me as well. That is the lesson.

Q: Is that detachment?

B: That is part of being detached.

Q: Then it seems simpler to me not to come here any more.

B: No, the lessons you are receiving here cannot be acquired in Holland at the same pace. This yearning belongs to the process. That has to be brought home to you, as said before.

39
BEYOND TIME

4 September 1995
Back again in Holland

Following a dream in which Baba confronts me again with the fact that in general He only gave me repeated short looks in the Ashram.

Question: Those looks were really meant for me then, but I wasn't sure?

Baba: Yes.

Q: Why couldn't it have happened a little more obviously?

B: It is not the intellect that judges what is good for you and what isn't. It is the integrated knowledge, BEING, existence, which responds alertly to every situation and which takes from it whatever it has to offer.

Q: And that is quicker than the intellect, it seems.

B: Yes, it is beyond the intellect, it is something which takes place outside of time. It places time off-side, as it were. Thinking requires time, this goes faster than thinking and therefore, in retrospect, it seems not to be meant for you, because then you are again in the thought-process of reasoning out things.

Q: But what good is it to me, if I don't know that You are looking at me from afar?

B: That which is beyond the intellect, knowledge by itself, does not need time. The duration of a look from you to me is again such a time-experience. If it happens beyond time, the duration of my look at you is totally unimportant.

Q: But still, sometimes You do look for a long time.

B: Then I fall in with your wishes, which have been anchored in time.

Q: Am I trying to go beyond that? Is that the reason why You didn't look long at me anymore?

B: You must learn to go beyond that, I am teaching it to you.

Q: I surely am a slow learner.

B: It is quite difficult for those who live in time to judge things by their timeless value. Do not feel guilty about it. Accept that it is a learning process, which cannot be acquired from one day to the next.

40
SHIVA/SHAKTI

4 September 1995

Following a dream

Baba: Shiva is the state of Being, Shakti is the action which belongs in the state of Being.

Question: Then Shiva/Shakti is not animus/anima?

B: No, animus is Shiva/Shakti and anima is Shiva/Shakti.

Q: I read somewhere that Shiva is the immovable, the observer, and that Shakti represents action, Creation.

B: There is no difference between Shiva and Shakti. They are aspects of the same. Shiva/Shakti is Shiva. Shakti is the energy of Shiva, Shiva is the whole.

Q: Is it the same as Purusha/Prakriti?

B: Not entirely. Purusha is Atma. Prakriti is Creation. Shiva/Shakti is Purusha plus Prakriti. Shiva/Shakti is the dance of Shiva ànd the dancer ànd the effect of the dance. Shiva/Shakti is the energy of Purusha. Shakti is not without Shiva. Shiva is not without Shakti. Shakti is the energy aspect of Shiva. Shiva is the totality: energy and existence.

Q: But isn't existence energy?

-No answer

Q: Can You explain that to me, Baba?

B: I can explain, but words are not sufficient. Existence is energy, but also that which goes beyond energy. Existence is actually also immobility, absolute quiet, absolute motionlessness.

Q: Is that also energy?

B: That is the highest form of energy.

Q: Is the motion then so rapid that immobility appears?

B: No, immobility is then so concentrated that it includes motion.

Q: Is that something different?

B: Yes, it goes beyond motion.

Q: Does it go beyond Creation then, for in Creation everything is in motion, isn't it?

B: Yes, it was what was before Creation.

Q: So, that was a total immobility?

B: Yes.

Q: And that was Shiva?

B: That is Shiva.

Q: Without Shakti?

B: No, Shakti and Shiva are one, they cannot be seen separate from each other.

Q: Then motion and motionlessness are one?

B: Yes.

Q: Is that the final unity beyond time?

B: Yes, that is timelessness which contains in itself time and with it Creation.

Q: What is the use of knowing this?

B: There is no use, it is as it is.

Q: To me it seems that this knowledge is impenetrable. I want to know and at the same time it gets me nowhere.

B: It is abstract knowledge, which elevates you to a higher plane of existence.

Q: But it doesn't have a practical use?

B: Everything that elevates a person has a practical use.

Q: But can I apply it in my life?

128

B: No, that happens by itself. Watch your dreams. Listen to your dreams. Look around you. Look at the motionlessness in motion. Experience motion in motionlessness.

Q: For instance when I look at a table, it is actually an enormous whirling of molecules and atoms?

B: Yes.

Q: And when I look at the wind through the trees, that is actually the immobility of unity, of the state of unity which changes from second to second, of which You spoke before?

B: Yes.

Q: So, actually immobility and motion are one?

B: They are one, but not on the basis of the examples you just gave. There you speak about two different things.

Q: But also in those molecules/atoms which whirl around in the table, there is - or there should be - one billionth of a second every time that everything stands still, isn't there?

B: No, there never is. Everything stands still, precisely because there is never immobility, only motion.

Q: Is that the dance of Shiva?

B: Yes.

Q: So, when I want to be completely still within myself, that only will happen when I realize that everything is always continuously in motion?

B: Yes, yes.

Q: Are those the vibration levels, of which You spoke before? (see lesson 28)

B: The vibration levels I spoke about were those of consciousness. These are motions as well, but not of Creation, of the material world, but of that which was before Creation, before time. So, essentially it is not the same.

Q: But for instance vibration levels of sound or colours?

B: Vibrations of sound and colours and such have to do with waves that are independent of matter. What is dependent on matter and therefore on time, is the channel to receive these waves.

129

Q: So, these waves by themselves also existed before time, before Creation?

B: Yes.

Q: In the form of the primal sound "OM"?

B: Yes.

Q: That was all there was then?

B: That is still all there is.

Q: So, actually there is no difference between what was before Creation and what is now?

B: No, it is all one.

Q: But You have said, "I have divided myself from myself to experience myself"

B: That is correct.

Q: So, then there was a moment before Creation?

B: Man is God. Creation divided itself from itself in the form of God, to experience itself.

Q: So, Creation has as much divided itself into that what was before Creation to experience God, as God divided Himself from Himself to experience Creation?

B: That's what it all comes down to.

Q: So, there was no beginning and there is no end?

B: Precisely.

Q: Is there more, Baba or is this it?

B: There is more.

Q: I have no questions anymore, Baba, this is already very difficult to understand.

B: There is more in the sense that having no beginning and no end equally means that everything begins and ends. No beginning and no end is motionlessness. Every beginning and every end is motion. This is what motion implies.

Q: Can I take this quite literally? For instance, I get up, start doing something, stop doing it or I am born, live and die again?

B: Yes, You can also see it in the sub-atomic world. Particles are and stop being.

Q: But what is it then that is "without beginning and end"?

B: In the unity where everything takes place at the same moment, all this exists without beginning and end.

Q: What good is it to me to know this?

B: Nothing and everything. Continue living. Live each day as if it is finite, but know that every end implies a new beginning. A new day is approaching.

Q: And the night?

B: The deep sleep is the state of unity without beginning and end. A continuous state of BEING, a merging with the Void which is All.

Q: But if we don't know this, it may as well not be there?

B: One day you will know where you are then. When consciousness and merging become one, bliss will consciously be your share.

Q: I find it very complicated, Baba.

B: It is very simple, as long as you do not think about it. Undergo it and trust.

Q: Trust what?

B: My omniscience, my support, me.

Q: Thank You, Baba. I would like to write more, but I have the feeling that it is to no avail.

B: Why not?

Q: Because I end up in some kind of circle, I repeat myself.

B: You are not in a circle, but in a spiral.

Q: Will it ever reach heaven?

B: Yes.

Q: Does heaven exist?

B: Heaven is the bliss that is the heritage of all of you. From where you have originated and where you will return to again.

Q: Is this Jnana (knowledge), this trying to find out?

B: This is Jnana coupled to Bhakti (devotion). An opening-up of yourself to reveal the knowledge that is inside you.

Q: Is this knowledge inside me or do You give it to me?

B: There is no difference.

41
WHY WE GET CHILDREN

22 September 1995

Following an incident, in which someone got something from Baba that I would like to have received myself. Although I was happy for the other person, I was sad at the same time, because such a thing didn't seem to be given to me. When I ask Baba for advice, He gives me among other things the following answer:

Baba: You would want anything for your daughter, wouldn't you? More so than you would want it for yourself?

Question: Yes, for her I would.

B: Regard the others as your children, then it will be easier for you.

Q: But how do I do that?

B: Think of your daughter, of what you would like her to have. Put your daughter every time in the place of the fellow human being with whom you are dealing.

Q: So, when I have a conversation with one friend or an other, I picture the face of my daughter with it?

B: Yes, you could do that.

Q: Are there other possibilities then?

B: Yes, you could also picture the character of your daughter with it.

Q: Then I will automatically feel the love I have for her?

B: No, that is not the way to word it, try again.

Q: Then I will be glad when others have the things I would like for my daughter and I will be sincerely happy when something happens to them in relation to You?

B: That's it.

Q: So, when I hear others talk about something special, I should imagine that it is my daughter who is telling me this?

B: Yes, that is precisely what it is all about.

Q: Isn't that very difficult?

B: It is a matter of exercise and of putting it into practice, in the long run it will happen automatically, and all will be your children.

Q: Why is it, concerning things that have to do with You, easier to be sincerely glad without thinking of myself when it involves my daughter?

B: Because you regard her as part of yourself and you accept her as such. In the same way you should regard and accept all as part of yourself.

Q: Is that why we get children, in order to learn this?

B: That is partly so, but that is not the only reason, of course. Children are born to perpetuate humanity. The former reason, however, does also exist. Children can teach man what love for others implies.

Q: Are there also other reasons?

B: There are several other reasons.

Q: Are they also born with us because of a mutual Karmic bond?

B: That is also possible. A child is always born in a specific family for a complex of reasons which are all interrelated.

Q: Have all births been chosen consciously?

B: Not all, that depends on the degree of consciousness of the individual.

Q: So, we should regard others as our children?

B: Yes.

42
WORK

Question: Baba, why can't we just be happy that we have helped another person without expecting recognition from that person. Is that insecurity?

Baba: When you can be ego-less, not expecting anything from people anymore, you will get recognition.

Q: But then that isn't important to us anymore.

B: Not to the ego. But it will please you to have made another person happy.

Q: Is that what it is always about?

B: For everyone who is a public figure, who works in public, that should be what it is about. That is the step which goes beyond insecurity. However, most people who work for others, in whatever respect, need recognition to prove themselves, to become surer of themselves. They do not realize that security must come from inside, from the Atma, from God. Security has been hidden by layers of ignorance, by conditioning, by wrongly acquired habits in one's youth and thus insecurity is maintained and people find themselves in the vicious circle of wanting recognition in order to conquer their insecurity, which will never happen that way. On the contrary, the insecurity will only grow because of it. For each small rejection will count many times more than whatever amount of approval. Only when the desire to prove oneself in this manner has diminished, can real security be rediscoverd, revealed.

Q: You have said that we must go from self-sacrifice to self-satisfaction to self-confidence to self-realisation.

B: Yes, those are the steps.

Q: Then what about people who appear in public?

B: Appearing in public is in the first instance an act of self-sacrifice. One gives of oneself, without being aware of it, it is true, but even so it is a giving of oneself. One subjects oneself to criticism and one goes beyond the limitations of being enclosed by the body. One presents an act of courage to the world.

Q: But isn't it true that people often appear in public to get recognition?

B: No, it isn't till later that this need arises. In the first instance it is truly an act of effacing oneself.

Q: Yes, yes and by doing so a person becomes contented with himself, gets self-satisfaction?

B: No, it is different, the Self is contented.

Q: It is about the Self then, the Higher Self?

B: Of course.

Q: Was that also the case with self-sacrifice?

B: Yes, you sacrifice, as it were, your lower self to the Higher Self.

Q: Is this only valid for people who appear in public?

B: What do you understand by that?

Q: Well, for instance artists, or also social assistants.

B: It goes further than that. Every work is an act in public and can be seen as self-sacrifice, an offer to the Supreme. A going beyond the limitations of the body. To work is to serve God. There is no work to which that rule doesn't apply. Working is a sacrifice to God.

Q: But not every sort of work takes place in public.

B: Public means that it can be seen, by how many is not relevant. It can bear the light of day, it meets the norms.

Q: So, for instance domestic work is also counted in this respect?

B: Of course.

Q: But You have often said that the fruit of one's work is not important.

B: It isn't, that is not what it is about, it is about the work in itself. The willingness to make a sacrifice. The result you leave to the Lord.

Q: But doesn't one have to do things as well as possible?

B: Of course, your sacrifice to Him must be optimal, that is the very reason that you need not worry about the result. If you act to the best of your ability, it is good, isn't it?

Q: Yes. So, the work, whatever it is that we do, is the step of self-sacrifice. In return, the Higher Self receives satisfaction?

B: That's how you could put it.

Q: Then it isn't entirely like that?

B: No, it goes further, in return you receive satisfaction of the entire being.

Q: But it wasn't about the result?

B: Not in advance. However, the result is the fruit of your work dedicated to God and given back again by Him to you as a gift. The result is the basis for further work, for new work, once again dedicated to Him.

Q: And that way it always goes on?

B: Yes, that way everything renews itself continuously.

Q: But why isn't self-confidence there right away then? You would think, if you are satisfied with your work and if you have satisfied your Self, that that is self-confidence?

B: Optimally it is. The problem is that man remains caught in desires. His desires play him false. His satisfaction is of short duration, he wants more and better all the time, he forgets that the work was a sacrifice to God. He regards the work as his achievement and longs for admiration from others and fame. The inner satisfaction is no longer a compensation, is no longer sufficient for him. He loses sight of it or considers it unimportant.

Q: Yes, yes, that I understand and instead of experiencing that inner satisfaction as a great good, he now wants recognition from others and if he doesn't get it, he becomes more and more insecure?

B: That is correct.

Q: But how does he escape from that?

B: By going back to his starting point, by regarding his work as a sacrifice to God and by considering the satisfaction it gives as the reward for his work. What another person thinks of it or doesn't is not important. What is important is what he himself thinks of it, what God thinks of it.

Q: Yes, for God and man are one.

B: That's it.

Q: And only then, when you can be satisfied in that way, when you can live in that way with everything you do, are you on the point of going towards self-realisation?

B: You don't go towards it consciously, it is an automatic follow-up of living according to the guidelines just mentioned. From self-confidence arises self-realisation. I speak then of self-confidence for a full hundred per cent, always and everywhere, whoever or whatever injures you no matter how, no matter how much you are slandered and despised. And the latter is a reality, the greater the self-confidence, the closer to self-realisation, the more the world will resist. That is a pattern. Do not blame the world for it, it can't act otherwise. No, see it as a test; how great is your self-confidence? Are you really unwavering in yourself, or do you let the world pull you down? Are you capable of experiencing the negativity of another person as something positive, because in the last resort it will make you stronger? Can you forgive in that way? Love the other person for his meanness, because that is the very thing that will make you grow? You see what it is all about in the long run?

Q: Yes, I understand. Actually it all ties up very beautifully and that is the way in which it makes sense to love our enemies, as Jesus wants from us. We then love our enemies because they, more than our friends, help us to reach self-realisation.

B: Yes, that's what it is all about. Recognize it. Be thankful to them and that way you can love them eventually.

Q: Yes, I have experienced that. There was this woman who was quite nasty to me and my inner reaction was not very nice. Suddenly I saw what I was doing and I realized that it was precisely because of her nastiness that I was able to watch myself and see that I was not quite as forgiving as I would like to be.

B: Precisely, that's the whole point. This woman has therefore rendered you a tremendous service by showing you something about yourself that would have stayed hidden otherwise. You can be thankful to her and a next step is to love her.

Q: Yes, I can do that in theory, for it makes a lot of sense. Whether I can do it when I meet her again, I don't know, we shall see about that when the occasion arises.

B: That is good, let it rest. It is about the mechanism and you understand now how it works. To love is not something that you can command at any moment and it is also not important that it is "in deed" carried out towards every so-called "enemy". To love means as well not to remain with a grudge but to recognize that the other person has helped you to grow, precisely because of his inimical deed.

Q: Yes Baba, that is really fantastic, if one could live like that, everything would be really perfect.

B: What stops you?

Q: I think that I stop myself. For it is not always immediately recognisable.

B: What is not recognisable?

Q: Actually I myself am not immediately recognisable. It means that I have to watch myself very closely, my reactions to everything and everyone.

B: Precisely, that's what it is about, that is the only thing that counts. Who are you? How do you react? Where are your good and your bad qualities. Notably the hidden bad qualities. The other person is your mirror. Love him for it.

Q: Is that what we all are to one another?

B: Yes. That is the function of human relationships.

Q: It seems so simple suddenly, for if, as soon as someone acts nastily, you would ask yourself right away, "How do I react? What do I feel now? What would I most want to reply or rather not?", you are not at all occupied with the nastiness of that other person anymore and it doesn't interest you anymore either

B: Correct. In the long run there is no other at all actually. There is only God. In you and in that other person. God who shows himself to you through that other person, shows your Self to you.

I keep thinking about it and after having done some things in the house, I return to it.

Q: So, self-sacrifice is not effacing yourself for an-other?

B: No, self-sacrifice is effacing yourself for your Self. For Him, for God. Doing things freely, without expecting a reward, just doing everything to the best of your ability taking into account the five human values.

Q: Please let me recapitulate: You begin with self-sacrifice, which is working without expecting a reward, without attaching importance to the result. Working for work's sake. Dedicating it to God and leaving the rest to Him. And everything you do conscientiously and to the best of your ability can be regarded as work then?

B: That's how it is.

Q: That provides satisfaction for both the lower and the Higher Self and by being really satisfied with it and really not longing for recognition or caring what other people think of you and your work, you reach self-confidence. Confidence of the lower self in the Higher Self, the Atma.

B: Yes, that's right.

Q: And then you can reach Self-realisation without consciously striving for it?

B: That is correct. Every act of striving keeps you away from God. In its place comes a certainty that God will grant you the grace of self-realisation when the time is right.

Q: Yes, for everything is right, so self-realisation or not doesn't actually matter anymore then.

B: No, the one is the other. Self-realisation is in fact the complex of all these things, of self-sacrifice, self-satisfaction and self-confidence. They reinforce each other. Not only do they lead to self-realisation, they áre already, as it were, self-realisation, only not consciously put into words.

Q: But I have read somewhere that a realised person cannot live for more than 21 days on earth.

B: These are matters you need not worry about. These things have always been said in a certain context. Besides, there are gradations of self-realisation. For that matter, the question itself shows that self-realisation has not taken place, for it implies a wanting to know. Break away from that. How long you or anybody else will live on earth is something God decides. And being realised or not, has not a great deal to do with it.

Q: It has to some degree then?

B: Certainly. However, we talk here in terms of lives and not in terms of years.

Q: Are there realised people who have stayed alive for more than 21 days?

B: Of course there are, many even.

Q: So, it is not true.

B: That's not what I said. Again, let it be. What you and everyone else can work at, are the steps leading up to and including self-confidence. The rest you leave to Him, to God, to your Self.

I just returned from shopping and on my way I thought "So, you don't efface yourself for others, but for the Self, for your Higher Self", and then it seemed as if Sai Baba said, "Effacing yourself for others would of course be very wrong indeed".

Q: Why then, Baba?

B: Because it might be your Higher Self that is effaced. Efface yourself for the Higher Self, then you know for sure that your Higher Self is preserved for you and, as a matter of fact, that way you help others most, for eventually there is only one Higher Self.

Q: But Baba, surely we know whether it is our Higher Self or our lower that we efface?

B: That's just it, you often have no idea. With most of your acts you don't know whether it is for the Self or whether lower impulses are causing you to act for the sake of the ego, the non-Self that is.

Q: How come we don't know this?

B: Because of the veiling of Maya. Because the Self is concealed in the world of phenomena. Because the world of phenomena is seen as the Self. What makes it all the more confusing is that this is partly true. The world of phenomena is also the Self. It depends on your perception of it.

Q: What do You mean by that?

B: When you perceive the Higher Self - the Atma - from your Higher Self - the Atma - then everything you see is the Self.

Q: That is the way You look at things? (see lesson 24)

B: Yes, that is how I perceive things.

Q: And when we look at things that way, we look at the Self?

B: Yes.

Q: But surely we don't always know that then?

B: Only I know how and from which motive you look at things. The Self knows it, but the veiling can be such that you don't know it. You are then immersed in the veiling-process to such a degree that it is totally unclear to you, what or who looks, despite the fact that it is very well possible that you perceive from the Higher Self - the Atma. Only God knows this; God looks at the hearts of people, not at their deeds. God sees through the motives. You often have no insight into it; hence the confusion, the doubt that prevails, often with spiritually oriented people.

Q: But why is that so, why have You made it so confusing?

141

B: It is inherent to the Atmic principle. The confusion will be removed when you don't ask yourself anything anymore. Do not bother about who acts, your ego or your Higher Self. Act with the human values in mind and trust that by working that way, you let God work in you. Leave the rest to Him.

Q: Yes, yes, then we have returned again to self-sacrifice, doing things without bothering about the result, only doing everything as well as possible.

B: That is correct.

Q: But surely effacing yourself for others that way must be good?

B: Since, as said before, you do not fully know what you are effacing, it is not sensible. Efface yourself for yourself, for your Self. That is real self-sacrifice. You efface yourself then for the Self, the Self in you and in others. For God.

Q: And the way we do that is by dedicating everything we do to You without worrying about the result?

B: That is the way to God, to the Self, to Self-realisation. Know that you and all other selves form together the Self. The One is the multiplicity and the multiplicity is the One.

Q: How can that be?

B: It can, but it cannot be explained by natural science?

Q: What do You mean by that?

B: It cannot be explained by the laws of physics as they are now known.

Q: Can it ever be explained by the laws of physics?

B: Much will be explained, but new, elusive facts will always present themselves, as long as man focusses physics on the material world. When man looks at processes in physics from the Atma, the Self, and also when the Self is observed from the newly established laws which go beyond the material world, a new process pattern of understanding will arise.

Q: What do You mean by that?

B: Things can be explained on the basis of laws of process patterns, other laws, however, than the ones known so far. Atma knows everything and is everything. Atma is inherent to itself. To the Self. Differences and discrepancies will be solved in one moment of omniscience. Again and again. That's what man is destined for.

Q: The scientist also?

B: Especially the scientist. A completely new branch of science will arise and the scientists of the old stamp will join in, because the pieces of the puzzle will all fall into place.

Q: Was the old science for nothing then?

B: Nothing is for nothing. They were building-blocks in the whole. Without the one no understanding of the other could - can - come about.

Q: But Atma knows everything?

B: The person who focusses on the Atma and looks from the Atma, doesn't - didn't - need those building-blocks. The scientist, however, who wants to approach things from the world of phenomena, will not be able to reach an all-embracing conclusion and solution at the same time without a logical progression of things - logical for him that is. Besides, it was work in which one was effacing oneself, where one was absorbed in making discoveries for the benefit of science, so in the long run this cannot but contribute to the benefit of the whole.

Q: But it was not work in which the result did not matter.

B: In a certain sense it was - is. One was contented with a small part of the eventual great whole and realised quite well that the great whole was too far away and too elusive to grasp. In that respect the scientist has proven to be capable of self-sacrifice.

Q: And the other steps to come to self-realisation?

B: Self-satisfaction is the point where many got stuck, for satisfaction was felt and reached for the benefit of the ego and not for the benefit of the Self. This is the big stumbling-block, notably for those who are not spiritually inclined. Precisely when one chooses the spiritual path, one realises that it is not about the ego, about self-interest, about one's own gain. That it is indeed about the Self, that the ego forms an obstruction in this process. It stands in the way of reaching the high goal.

Q: Yes in this day and age it all seems to revolve around the glorification of the ego, you actually see that in all fields of work.

B: Precisely, that is the tendency of the Kali Yuga. The ego is placed upon a pedestal and the Self is forgotten. Eventually that will lead to pain and suffering and the fall of humanity.

Q: Is that why You have come on earth?

B: Yes, to reverse this fate is the task of the Avatar, the promise of the Avatar.

Q: As You promised, as Krishna, in the Bhagavad Gita, "Whenever Dharma (righteousness) is in decline and evil rules, I manifest. To protect the good, to destroy the wicked and to establish righteousness I manifest from eon to eon". (Bhagavad Gita 4, verses 7 and 8)

B: Yes, that is the promise I have kept for the preservation of humanity.

Q: Krishna is Baba and Baba is Krishna?

B: Yes, there is no difference.

Q: And we are allowed to recognise You?

B: I am recognisable for everyone, but look from the Atma, from the Higher Self.

Q: Yes of course, and those people that recognise You, or have recognised You, have looked in that fashion, even though they were not always aware of it?

B: Exactly, that is what we talked about. Man often doesn't know whether he acts, looks, experiences from the ego or from the Self.

Q: How can he become aware of it?

B: By acting with the five human values (Truth, Righteousness, Inner Peace, Love and Non-violence) in mind and by testing everything by them. That way he knows that he is on his way to purity and that he has acted to the best of his knowledge. The rest he leaves to God. God judges and reviews, man works for God and has trust.

Q: And what about God's grace then?

B: Gods grace is poured out upon those who act in confidence, who have confidence in the Self, who have Self-confidence.

Q: But isn't Self-confidence in itself grace already?

B: Yes, eventually all is grace. Though only he will realise this, who has confidence in God, who has confidence in the Self.

Q: Is, in fact, seeing everything as grace the highest grace?

B: Precisely, then you are a person without desires.

Q: Then even ugly and nasty behaviour towards oneself - yes, even war - can be seen as grace?

B: Yes, now you have arrived at the starting point of your question. That is the whole point. When we have come that far, we are realised.

Q: Why do you say "we" now?

B: Because I enter intensively into the life of each human being. There is no difference. God is man, man is God. On that level, the level of self-realisation, there is "we". Not "I", not "He", but "we". And "we" is one. One "we". One humanity. One world. One cosmos.

43
PRAYERS ARE NOT ALWAYS ANSWERED

2 November 1995

I am translating one of Baba's discourses and suddenly I get the feeling that He wants me to ask Him a question.

Question: Do you want me to start writing, Baba?

Baba: Yes.

Q: But I don't have any questions.

B: Yes, you do.

Q: Is it in connection with what I just translated, "You may give all your pain and sorrow to Him, but it should never be feigned, then you will get nothing in return"?

B: Yes.

Q: But I believe that, what should I ask about that?

B: You should take it to heart.

Q: Yes, that makes sense to me, for I remember that once in Your Whitefield ashram I was suddenly sad about the fact that back home in Holland I never have the experience of the appearance of Your form or of hearing Your actual voice, but at the same time I felt that I wasn't really sad about it. That it was play-acting. That I very much wanted it - and still do - but I wasn't bowled over with sorrow about it. Is that what You mean?

B: Yes.

Q: But that doesn't happen very often with me, does it? When there is something the matter with me, it usually is true, or not?

B: In your case, yes.

Q: Not in the case of others, then?

B: No.

Q: How is that?

B: They think they come with their problems, but all those underlying layers are not broached.

Q: You mean that they project their real sorrow onto superficial things and then come to You with that?

B: Yes.

Q: But if they don't know any better, they can't help it, can they?

B: That is true; they are, however, surprised when God doesn't answer their prayers. God doesn't answer their prayers because what they ask for is not what they really want.

Q: So, a person should first really look deep inside before asking You for something?

B: Yes.

Q: But when someone is ill, for instance, and asks You to cure him, then isn't that a legitimate question?

B: Not always.

Q: How is that then?

B: Illness can be a means of hiding behind a still greater evil, a way out of even more misery.

Q: And if such a person asks You for a cure and You would grant that, then the underlying evil would come to light, which would be much worse for that person?

B: Yes.

Q: So, one is not allowed to ask for healing?

B: It is allowed; however, man should not be worried or turn away from me if what he asks for is not answered or granted.

Q: I get the feeling that it bothers You that this happens, that You find it disagreable.

B: I am not bothered about anything when it concerns myself. However, I would like to spare people pain and sorrow by making them see that when their prayers are not answered, it is for their own good. They can do two things then: either accept what happens to them cheerfully, or realise that there must be something else in them which keeps their prayers from being answered.

Q: What is better?

B: Self-knowledge advances man more. Acceptance, however, shows that man's trust is great. So, there is no "better". Both things can exist independent of each other or together.

Q: So, if someone is ill and, despite his prayers, You don't heal him, then the best procedure is 1. acceptance of that illness or 2. trying to discover the underlying cause of that illness and then giving that problem to You?

B: Yes.

Q: And that problem will be heard by You then?

B: If that problem is real, true, and if it is placed before me in truth, it will be answered, always.

Q: And if one would only accept being ill, but not try to find out the underlying reasons?

B: Then the gain is that this person can be happy in spite of the illness that befalls him. Such a person is a real devotee. He doesn't ask questions, he accepts.

Q: So, he is more advanced?

B: No, you cannot speak in those terms. The difference is the path he walks. One person walks the path of devotion, bhakti-yoga, the other that of knowledge, jnana-yoga.

Q: And both paths lead to God?

B: Yes, eventually they do.

Q: And they are linked together as well?

B: That is correct. Devotion leads to true knowledge. True knowledge leads to devotion.

Q: Is it important for people to know this?

B: Yes.

Q: Why?

B: Because not knowing this keeps many from finding me.

Q: Is it that they turn away from You, because their prayer is not answered?

B: That's right.

Q: So, it is actually very simple, the way I understand it now. If your prayer is not answered, you can do two things: 1. you accept it and you accept what happens to you, and doing so you walk the path of bhakti-yoga, devotion. 2. You start discovering that that wasn't the real problem you wanted to give to God and you are going to try to find out what was. Then you walk the path of jnana-yoga, knowledge.

B: Yes.

Q: Is that all, Baba?

B: That is all. This had to be said, because it confuses many people.

Q: Baba, may I just relate this to myself?

B: Go ahead.

Q: I am faced with some kind of problem, which is that I don't know how to decide my attitude anymore in respect of certain people, who behave in a rather blunt and unfriendly way towards me. So, now I can either accept that they are as they are, or I can try to find out what is the underlying motivation. Should I look at *my* underlying motivation then, why it disturbs *me*?

B: No, that is not the problem. You have established an objective fact.

Q: So, I should look at *their* underlying motivation?

B: Yes.

Q: Should I also accept *their* attitude then and not *mine*?

B: Yes of course, in this case that is the acceptance which is relevant here. It has nothing to do with you, in fact.

Q: So, I either accept them the way they are with their shortcomings, or I try to find out what lies behind it?

B: Yes.

Q: When I do the former, I am practising bhakti-yoga and when I do the latter, am practising jnana-yoga?

149

B: Yes.

Q: So, you don't need to apply this only to yourself, you can also apply it to others?

B: Always, at all times, with everything that presents itself.

Q: I think I know the underlying reason in their case, but even though I know it, I still cannot accept it.

B: Why not?

Q: I find it so very narrow-minded of them. I can imagine that someone's first reaction is like that, but couldn't they get over it? It has been going on for two weeks now.

B: You could also get over it.

Q: Yes, but I am confronted with it again and again.

B: No, your acceptance is not yet optimal and at the same time there is no real understanding of *their* underlying problems.

Q: Yes that is true, Baba.

B: And as to them, something like that can last a long time. However, that is their process. All you need is to understand it.

Q: I do understand, Baba, but I cannot manage to have any love for it, I cannot really accept it.

B: That is what you should work at.

Q: At other times it seems to me that there is acceptance - it is the only thing I can do - but no understanding.

B: Acceptance is not a matter of accepting the situation because there is nothing else one can do. That is fooling yourself. Acceptance in respect of another person is accepting the other person with his faults, completely losing sight of these faults, forgetting them, as it were.

Q: And if I can't do that, it is better to look at why they do it?

B: Yes, that is the faster way in such a case. By understanding why, you can often still come to acceptance.

44
THOUGHTS

15 December 1995

I am reading something about the speed of light and I lapse into reflection. I remember that Baba once let me know that there is indeed something faster than light, and that is thought.

Question: Is this so, Baba?

Baba: Yes.

Q: But when I conceive a sentence, doesn't that take longer than the time light needs to travel?

B: When you think of me, I know this and I am with you.

Q: But isn't this because You already live in us?

B: Yes and no. I live inside you, but my physical form in Puttaparthi has also knowledge of it. For that matter, this same phenomenon holds good for every human being in relation to someone else. Only people don't know this, they are not receptive to someone else's thoughts which reach man at a subconscious level, both good and bad thoughts.

Q: Is that why black magic works?

B: Yes. But in the long run this black thought-power will always have a retroactive effect on the one who expressed the thoughts or rather thought them.

Q: Is that why thoughts are as important as actions? I have come upon that in Your writings and also in the writings of other masters.

B: Thoughts are as powerful as actions, but their effect on other people can be crystallized out sooner.

Q: What do You mean by that?

B: It is always a process of choice, no matter whether something comes to someone by thought or action. The choice of following up someone else's action and to set to work with it takes more time than picking up someone else's thought because here the choice doesn't occur consciously, but at a subconscious level. By crystallizing-out I mean that at all times a process of taking shape occurs, a lasting change in the other person. This is, as it were, the growth-process of consciousness. With physical growth it is matter that is crystallized out, with spiritual growth it is subtle energy.

Q: But isn't the body fully grown at a certain moment, and all there is left then is a break-down of cells?

B: Cells keep renewing themselves constantly. What is broken down is the most crude matter; it weakens slowly but surely.

Q: So, when I think of someone, it doesn't matter how great the distance is between that person and me, it always strikes a chord in the other person, even though he has no conscious knowledge of it?

B: Yes.

Q: Is that the reason why it is important to think only good thoughts about and towards the other person?

B: Thinking good thoughts is better than thinking bad thoughts. Not thinking, unless there is a necessity for it, is better still.

Q: What do You mean by that?

B: When a problem needs to be solved, this requires thought. The work you do requires thought. Your intellect in combination with Buddhi (the capacity for discrimination), brings about the highest kind of thoughts. Thinking about others without being asked - whether they are good thoughts or bad - carries risks.

Q: But if they are good thoughts, why is that so?

B: Because, as said, such a thought reaches the other person faster than light and it will always somewhat change him.

Q: But when it is a good thought?

B: What do you understand by a good thought?

Q: For instance when I like somebody.

B: Such a thought is always subjective. The only kind of thought which might be - should be - sent disinterestedly and objectively to another person, is that

152

of light. Send light, love and peace to the other person. With it you send it into the cosmos where it will live on eternally.

Q: And those other thoughts, they will also live on eternally?

B: Nothing gets ever lost. However, they can be neutralized by light.

Q: Is that another reason why You advise us to do the light-meditation?

B: Yes, of course. We are light and every light-thought will transform the unconscious pull downward, will eventually dissolve it.

Q: But when I think, "so and so is such a nice person"?

B: It doesn't solve anything, it doesn't neutralize anything, it only adds to the confusion.

Q: Which confusion?

B: The confusion of words, of feelings, of one's own opinions.

Q: But sometimes it cannot be helped. Imagine you get a card from someone, isn't it logical then to think about that person?

B: Accept it for what it is and let go of it. At the moment that you receive the card the other person's process, his intention, has long been past. The actual moment of contact was the moment the other person got the impulse to send you the card. You responded to it unconsciously. When at the moment you receive the card you respond once again - consciously this time - it can be a reinforcement of the earlier impulse. In that case there is nothing wrong with it, but it is superfluous.

Q: And when the other person expects an answer?

B: Then we need a thought-process to come to action. To solve a particular problem, as it were. Then it is a creative process, which must be carried out.

Q: But in essence I already "knew" at the moment the other thought it?

B: Certainly.

Q: Then that's the reason that it is important to tune in to our inner knowledge, so that we can come up with the correct solution, or with the right answer?

B: Yes, all knowledge is already on hand.

Q: Still, sometimes it is nice to think of someone. You find a picture or a letter from someone and then this happens automatically.

B: There is nothing wrong with it; however, replace at such a moment your subjective opinion about the other person who evokes such thoughts in you, by light. Set to work on that consciously. Transform every thought about the other person through light.

Q: Also when I don't like the other person?

B: Precisely then. Not liking someone else is of course also subjective.

Q: But what if that other person has really done something bad?

B: Let it go, send light. Withdraw from it.

Q: From what, from the other person or from what he has done?

B: That depends on the relationship you have with that person and of the frequency of the incorrect behaviour. It is better to withdraw from people who repeatedly fall into the same mistake, without passing judgment.

Q: And what about a judge?

B: A judge fulfills a function within society. On the basis of his function, he will have to pass judgment and establish a sentence. However, a good judge will never end up in a personal relationship towards the other person. Society isn't served by that.

Q: Baba, are there other things faster than light?

B: Yes, the process of metamorphosis or the transformation-process.

Q: What do You mean by that?

B: It is, in fact, an extension of the previous. Everything another person picks up - consciously or unconsciously - transforms him. This transformation takes place at the same moment as the thought towards the other person, as the intention of a certain action towards the other person, and transforms that person through a crystallizing-out of that fact.

Q: And this goes faster than the speed of light?

B: Infinitely faster. It takes place, as it were, at the same moment.

Q: So, everything we think changes the earth as well as everything we do?

B: Every blade of grass that is picked gives the earth another look, each step that is made, each sentence that is written and therefore also each thought that is thought.

154

Q: But surely we can never escape it, this thinking I mean?

B: Nor is it necessary. This process of everlasting change implies the underlying unity which it is all about.

Q: You mean everything changes except the Atma, for the Atma IS, unchangeable, always.

B: Yes.

Q: Is it the Atma which brings about all these continuous changes?

B: No, the Atma is the spectator. Changing is inherent to matter. The moment matter is not subject to change anymore, it would cease to exist.

Q: Yes, that I understand; molecules, atoms, and so on, they are all in motion, it cannot be otherwise.

B: That's how it is, and the same goes for the energetic processes of thought and transformation and their attendant metamorphosis.

Q: Is that the same as transformation?

B: Yes, it implies the crystallization-process which repeats itself ad infinitum. Nothing is ever as it was before.

Q: And that goes faster than light?

B: It is one and indivisible, it happens without interruption and continuously. There is never one moment that something is not different from what it was before and the speed of these changes, brought about by the person himself or by the other person, is faster than the speed of light.

Q: But it is not perceptible to us.

B: Neither is the speed of light, only the results of it are perceptible.

Q: You just said that we should send light to the other person. Does this light travel with the speed of light?

B: No; here you come to the heart of the matter. The light of the Self, which we can send through our thoughts and which gives cause for transformation in the other person, travels through the thought-process, which - as we have seen is faster than the speed of light, in combination with the process of metamorphosis. Both travel faster than light travels. They are, however, part of the same process. The inner light, the light of the Atma, is faster than light on earth, because this light-source is of divine origin and God is light and is beyond the light. The light is from God. The light from the Atma is Atma, is God.

Q: So, when we send light towards the other person, we send God to him?

B: Yes, and as the other person is also God, the light reaches him at the same moment that it is sent.

Q: But bad thoughts also reach him right away, You said.

B: Yes, they obstruct however, the divinizing process, of both he who receives and he who is the sender.

Q: Is there more, Baba?

B: No, not for the moment.

45
THE DEATH-PROCESS

10 February 1996

Following a Baba-dream that I tried to interpret with His help.

Question: Did I interpret that dream correctly?

Baba: Partly.

Q: Why partly?

B: There is more.

Q: What then?

B: It is about the completeness of each experience.

Q: What do You mean by that?

B: The more completely an experience is integrated, the more one is ready for the death-process.

Q: You mean dying?

B: No, I mean living.

Q: You call life a death-process?

B: Yes.

Q: So, life is a process in order to die?

B: Isn't that evident?

Q: And the more completely we experience things, the more completely we go towards our death?

B: That is correct. And this does not only apply to this life. It applies to each life anew for everything we experience and go through.

Q: Until finally we die in a "good" way?

B: Until finally we die consciously. Until life and death have become one process of BEING. Until no distinction is made anymore between life and death.

Q: But does this also apply to the death of somebody else? When someone dear to us passes away, are we then also not allowed to make any distinction between life and death?

B: No, that has to do with the death-process - living one's life completely and integrating every experience - but not with dying. The physical death is something towards which we can only strive with our own consciousness. Someone else's death is an experience for us in the process of living, the death-process in other words. Our own death is the proof of the sum.

Q: The proof of whether we have integrated everything completely or not?

B: No, a death-process.

Q: Is there a difference?

B: The death-process is life itself. That is something else than the process of dying. The death-process is a process of living with death as its culmination. Earthly death to be sure. For nothing or nobody ever dies. There is One continuous existence.

Q: And that is the death-process?

B: No, the death-process is life here on earth which leads to an earthly death, an apparent death as we have seen. Which is, however, nothing else but one point in the eternal life; the life of the soul which knows no beginning or end.

Q: What makes the earthly death differ from the earthly life then?

B: It is like the difference between day and night. The point where one falls asleep can be compared to death. The body goes on living, however, and is there again on waking up the next day.

Q: But surely when we die, our body will never return again in that same form?

B: That is true, however that is only a matter of gradation. Our body which wakes up has also undergone changes, is no longer entirely the same as it was the day before. You can understand this when you look at the body of a child an adult and an elderly person and compare the three. The differences are greater than the similarities then.

158

Q: But doesn't this changing, this bodily growth or decay so to speak, also take place during the day? It doesn't have much to do, in fact, with our sleep, does it?

B: That is correct, it was meant as a comparison to show you that life is eternal and that death is only another form of life.

Q: But that is what makes it so uncertain for us, Baba. That we disappear as the person we are. That surely is quite different from falling asleep and waking up again, isn't it? Will You please shed some light on this for me, Baba?

B: When the analogy is taken too far, the clarity disappears.

Q: But what about this uncertainty then in which we people find ourselves in connection with death?

B: You must accept that. You must find a way to come to terms with that. Each man anew. And here again the question of integrating every experience plays a part. When we experience life consciously and accept it as it comes, the fact that we eventually die will be no problem whatsoever, because we have already seen it around us with loved ones who die. They are the very ones that have served as examples to us.

Q: But if their death was rather unpleasant?

B: Then they show us that eventually there is rest. And besides they teach us to accept what is unavoidable.

Q: So, dying has two functions? One for ourselves and one for the other person?

B: Dying has ultimately only one function, only the one for ourselves. That others can learn from it in the process, is a useful accidental circumstance, which has to do with the fact that here on earth interaction plays an important part. One thing is always connected with another, but eventually it is all about One Self (oneself!).

Q: Yes, I understand, we are all One, so whether I die or someone else doesn't make that much difference in the long run.

B: In the long run it doesn't, but it does as long as the death-process is still going on.

Q: With that You mean this life?

B: I mean the long line of lives which follow one another as the day follows the night.

Q: Does the complete integration of all events have to do with Karma-yoga?

B: Yes.

Q: Could You explain that?

B: Karma-yoga is doing things without bothering about the results. Living your life because it has been given to you. Accepting life as a gift. Living life as well as possible and seeing everything as God's will.

Q: We are part of God and God experiences through us that particular aspect of life?

B: That is a way to understand it.

Q: So, God must live life as well as possible?

B: No, God lives life as well as possible. That is what man should understand. Whatever happens is good, it is as God has willed it.

Q: I won't ask again about wars and diseases, for You have already spoken about them, but the fact is that it remains difficult.

B: Let it rest. Live. That is Karma-yoga. Live in the situation that presents itself to you. When it is less pleasant, you will trust God and deal with that situation adequately. You cannot do otherwise, can you?

Q: Then actually everthing we do is adequate. When someone screams out of misery or has sunk into dispair, as we see on the TV-news, is that adequate then for that situation?

B: Yes of course.

Q: But isn't that very gruesome?

B: It is as it is. Man does as he thinks fit, but God disposes.

Q: But all that cruelty results in people not being able to accept You.

B: When a judge passes judgement on a criminal, righteous judgement, and the criminal is taken to prison, do you consider that cruel?

Q: No, it serves him right.

B: And God is righteous?

Q: I think so.

B: Could it be then that that is what serves that person best?

Q: But Baba, when we look at people that way, aren't we very heartless? Where is our compassion then?

B: Beware, without compassion it is you who are that criminal, it is you who will be judged mercilessly. Always retain compassion. Let your heart melt again and again, each time you experience something as an injustice. Only, do not ask yourself why things happen. Accept that it is as it is and start acting adequately in keeping with what is within your reach.

Q: Then the horrors that happen to people are God's punishment?

B: That is incorrect for two reasons. In the first place the word "punishment" is out of place. "Corrective measure" would be better. Secondly it is not from God that the measure comes, but from man himself. It is his Self, the Atma, which has opted for this "measure".

Q: But isn't Atma God?

B: Yes, but Atma is also God in every human being. Through chastening a soul experiences itself and becomes aware of evil. However, there is something else. Horrors are often of a relatively short nature. Therefore, whoever judges such a person as being rightly punished by God knows a. no compassion and b. does not take in the whole at a glance, does not take in the healing effect of the "horror", which can even take place within one lifetime.

Q: So, when I see for instance images of homeless or hungry people on the TV-news, I do not need to wonder why God is so cruel, because it could very well be that it has a healing effect on that person and therefore there is no question of cruelty?

B: Yes, and you must look at it with his many lives in view; the accumulation of many lives has brought a person here to make him realize his mistakes, which often happens. Consult people who have gone through such ordeals. Not when they are in the middle of them, but when they have arrived at the next phase of their life and are capable of survey.

Q: But there are also many who don't make it, who die of starvation, exhaustion, cold?

B: When our starting-point is that death is a period of rest in the One life of many lives, then there is nothing wrong with that, is there?

Q: No, but what about the relatives then?

B: They will have to come to terms with this experience - the death-process, remember? The full integration of everything which presents itself in a lifetime.

Q: Yes, it all seems quite logical this way. But I keep finding all the suffering that goes with it unpalatable.

B: Have compassion. Don't call it unpalatable, just have compassion with what presents itself to you. Cruelties have been created by man and will have to be eradicated by man.

Q: You never meant it as cruel?

B: There is one ever-lasting life in which the divine sacrifices itself to God, surrenders itself as it were. The more resistance, the more difficult and cruel the struggle.

Q: But isn't surrender also cowardly?

B: Surrender to God is never cowardly. It is a deed of courage, a heroic deed. The more difficult the circumstance, the greater the heroism. The more one resists, the more difficult the circumstances become and therefore the greater the heroic deed. In that respect the most tortured person has the potential of becoming the greatest saint.

Q: And a criminal?

B: A criminal will first have to account for his deeds. As a tormented person, as a being who learns to have insight into the one, everlasting life, he will eventually reach saintliness.

Q: So, you can only reach saintliness, self-realisation, when you are tormented?

B: When you are chastened. This is usually spread over many lives, but no one can escape it.

Q: Can a person choose to take a great deal of suffering upon himself in one lifetime, in order to thus settle his debt rapidly?

B: That is possible and it happens.

Q: What about Jesus then?

B: Jesus is the perfect human being, who, as God's Son, has come to earth voluntarily to show man that suffering can be surmounted. His example can help many sufferers and does so indeed.

Q: And He also teaches us to have compassion?

B: Yes

162

Q: Baba, is there more?

B: There is more, but not for the moment.

I keep thinking about it and after a while I ask all the same:

Q: Doesn't Christ also show us that it is impossible for us to pass judgment about why someone suffers? Imagine we had said, "that must have been Karmic", we would have been totally wrong then.

B: That only confirms what was said before. Then you would not have had any compassion whatsoever. At the same time it shows that it is not up to man to judge. For no one knows why a particular suffering happens to a person. It can indeed be a chastening for certain bad behaviour. However, it can also be about a person who has chosen a particular suffering as a compensation for what another has done. In that case it is something holy. Since most people cannot assess this rightly, it is all the more reason not to pass judgment. Here again it is good to open yourself to compassion. This prevents wrong judgment from being made.

Q: Yes I understand, so what we must do when watching for instance the TV-news is to have compassion without asking any further questions.

B: Questions of a practical nature, "how can I help", or of a political nature, "how can a government help", are always adequate and therefore in place. Questions of a philosophical nature, "why does something have to happen to these particular people", seldom lead to correct understanding.

Q: They do exist though, people who understand?

B: Of course they do, however they do not ask questions but **see**.

Q: You mean they have insight into why things happen?

B: Yes.

Q: So, when we wonder in despair when seeing injustice, we should ask questions of a practical nature or not ask anything at all, is that what it all comes down to?

B: Yes. Offer help wherever possible, leave the rest to God. Focus on Him and continue with your life. Not with the life of those people you saw suffering on TV.

Q: And praying for them, is that allowed?

B: That is required, that is compassion which expresses itself in a form.

Q: But does it help?

B: Praying always helps. However, not always in the manner that man envisages. Pray and leave the rest to God. Praying for the salvation of the world is opening your heart to compassion and in consequence it will bring salvation to the world.

Q: If every human being would feel compassion at every moment, there would be no more suffering?

B: That is right.

46
THE HAPPINESS OF BEING

25 February 1995

I have come to the conclusion that the most important thing is to be constantly aware of God's presence. To know Him constantly around me, in me and with me. The way I experienced this once in Whitefield (India). That was actually very special. It was formless and at that time I couldn't fully accept it - yet. I wanted it to be Baba, but now I understand that it was formless because formlessness is the essence of the Supreme God. He can take on a form' if He so wishes, as in Baba. But actually He has done so in all of us. Only, Baba says, "I know that I am God, but you don't know". And I think that Baba means knowing it really, completely. Not just with your intellect, but with your entire being.

Question: Is this so, Baba?

Baba: Yes.

Q: Will we ever know it in this way, with our entire being?

B: Yes.

Q: Sometimes I feel You as love and warmth in my heart and in my arms, does that have to do with it?

B: Yes.

Q: But Ananda shouldn't become an end in itself, should it?

B: No. It is not about Ananda anymore. Ananda is a by-product; it belongs to the state of BEING, but BEING is more comprehensive.

Q: How do You mean that?

B: BEING comprises Ananda and non-Ananda. BEING is BEING One in God. BEING is God in you. BEING is One, undivided, indivisible, not to be separated.

Q: Still, I experience the world as separate from me.

B: The world does not exist. You exist, therefore the world exists.

Q: That I don't understand.

B: The world exists by the grace of the created. Atma IS and therefore the world exists.

Q: So, it is actually I who has created the world?

B: Yes.

Q: But I do not at all experience it as such.

B: That is because you identify yourself with your form. With whom you are now, in this incarnation. It is the Atma that has created the world. Identify yourself with the Atma and you will understand that you have created the world.

Q: Is it necessary to understand this?

B: No, absolutely not. Understanding will come, however. Only, everything in its own time. Do not ask yourself anything. Live and let God live in you.

Q: Is there more, Baba?

B: Yes, there is more, ask about happiness.

Q: What should I ask about happiness?

B: Ask what happiness is.

Q: What is happiness?

B: Happiness is the fact that you have a body. That you can and may realize God in the body. That is only given to man. Happiness is not something to be strived for. Happiness is to be a human being.

Q: You have said that the angels in the highest heavens long for that, is that true?

B: Yes.

Q: Why? They are so much more advanced than we are.

B: No, man is the highest divine creation. Man is equal to God. This can be said of none of the other creatures and beings.

Q: Is that why we have to suffer so?

B: Yes, that is the price that has to be paid.

Q: Why?

B: God can only be reached, when one is chastened by suffering, when the material world has been conquered by having lived through it. That requires great courage and the drive to conquer. Whoever takes that upon himself will be rewarded with invincibility, with Godliness.

Q: What about the angels then?

B: They form another part of the Divine plan. They will never become God, but be of service to man. The person who has become equal to God, to him the angels will be subservient.

Q: But isn't it true that angels can also become man?

B: Yes, that is possible.

Q: Do they also have to suffer then?

B: An angel among people must go through the suffering, just like everybody else. It is often even harder for such a person, because he is without guilt. It happens to him and he has no answer. He is pure and clean.

Q: Doesn't everyone think of himself as being pure and clean?

B: No, that is the mistake you make. Most people know very well that they are not.

47

A CHOICE BETWEEN GOOD AND GOOD

1 March 1996

All afternoon I have felt Baba very close to me and I wonder if He wants me to write.

Question: Baba, do You want me to write?

Baba: Yes.

Q: What about?

B: Consider what life is about.

Q: Isn't life about reaching God?

B: Yes.

Q: Is that what You want to communicate?

B: Yes.

Q: What then?

B: You must know that it lies in the predestination of the final process that I have come.

Q: What do You mean by that?

B: I have come on earth because it has been so preordained for the maintenance of the race of man.

Q: Would it perish otherwise?

B: Yes.

Q: Would it have massacred itself?

B: Not only that, natural disasters would have prevailed and would have destroyed the rest of humanity, those who would have been left.

Q: And this will not happen now?

B: This has been prevented by my Coming.

Q: Why do You want me to write about that?

B: Because knowing this will bring man closer to me. Man had better be aware of this. My Coming now influences millions, but it will influence billions.

Q: Will there be no natural disasters anymore then?

B: When all of mankind turns towards me - mind you, towards God - no natural disasters will take place anymore. Man will then live in harmony with himself and with the earth.

Q: Will Paradise be restored then?

B: Yes.

Q: But You have said before that this is an individual process which will not take place for everyone at the same time.

B: When enough people have reached this state of consciousness, the earth will be a Paradise. Those who have not acquired this consciousness will be dragged along then, this has also been said already.

Q: Yes, but what can we do about this, Baba? What good is it to know this?

B: You can co-operate in it. That's why you are on earth.

Q: How, Baba?

B: Open yourself to God. Let God, who you yourself are, work through you. Let Him pervade you. Let nothing keep you from being and remaining focused on the Self, on God in you. Let that be the message that resounds.

Q: But we often do not hear Your inner voice, even though we would like to. Then I really don't know what is the right thing to do, should I do this or that? Both seem Dharmic then, for evidently if something is A-dharmic, goes against Dharma, it is not good. But all those instances where it is not clear, how must we deal with them?

no answer

Q: Baba, won't You answer this question?

169

B: First start cooking, this will come later.

It has indeed inadvertedly become very late. I had just looked at my watch and thought, "actually I should stop."

4 March 1996

I read through the writings of 1 March and I ask myself if this is the moment to pursue that question.

B: Yes.

Q: Baba, the question was: how should we act when it is not always clear what You want from us. This or that, both seem good.

B: When both are good, then it is about making a choice. Act and do not worry about the result. Do not worry either about whether you have made the right choice or not. You have chosen according to the best of your conscience and that's what counts.

Q: But that other choice would also have been to the best of my conscience.

B: So be it. That is the essence of duality. Going from two to one is a difficult process. The choice seems up to you, but is eventually up to me.

Q: So, we must make a choice in such a case?

B: In any case. It is always about choices. The problem for you, however, is that it seems to be a choice between *good* and *good*. Choices between *good* and *bad* are easier in the long run; although it is not always clear to the person who is confronted with them, and if it is clear man is often not prepared to make a choice for good.

Q: Why not?

B: The ego often stands in the way here. The ego is eager for power, for its own gain, for fame and such. Once a person realises this and is able to make the right choices, the next step arises, a choice between two good things. Here it is no longer important *what* you choose, but *that* you choose. Living on earth requires action. Action is the making of choices.

Q: Yes, I understand, but the problem suddenly doesn't seem as urgent anymore as it was last Friday. I don't know what I wanted to know so badly then.

B: You and others would like God to decide everything. You would like it to be very clear what you must do in any circumstance, in any choice, since God —as the Other—whispers it to you. But you yourself are God. It is not the Other who takes you by the hand and tells you what to do. It is a certainty, a standing tall and remaining tall in anything you do. A making of choices in which the responsibilty lies fully in your hands. In which you cannot hide behind, "If only I had done that or acted in such a manner." You acted to the best of your knowledge and that makes it right.

Q: But when in retrospect another choice would have been better? For instance in retrospect it turns out that it would have been better to have bought something else, for the product I bought appears not to be sound?

B: Regard everything as a lesson. The next time you will consider the pros and cons even more attentively. That is all. It is about material things. Good or bad is not important. They are lessons in learning to focus the attention.

Q: Is that what making choices is?

B: Yes, it is being attentive, being attentively absorbed in everything and everyone.

Q: Is that consciousness?

B: That is optimal consciousness. Learning to deal with every situation. Eventually it will appear that choices form no dilemma any longer. Certainty will come in the place of doubt. Doing things with certainty, without worrying about the results thereof. Faultlessly adopting the right attitude.

Q: Is that how we can live with a heightened consciousness here on earth?

B: Yes. Doubt will diminish and knowing with absolute certainty that the choice is good, no matter how it turns out, will increase.

Q: It is as if you let God in you decide?

B: It *is* God in you who decides. However, He doesn't do it the way you expect, the way a child expects his parents to encourage him in making the right decisions. He does it by allowing you a free hand. As long as you cannot do that, you will get an indication from Him, provided that you focus on Him for a full hundred per cent. When your God-consciousness is optimal, you yourself will have to make the decisions. God and you overlap each other, there is no difference anymore. No other who advises you, it is you yourself. For you are the Self!

48
PAIN AND BLISS

21 April 1996

Last Sunday during the Bhajan-service in our center I felt bliss - His Ananda - in my heart and at the same time I felt a stinging pain to the right of my heart. It was pleasant and unpleasant at once. Very strange. At home this also continued. When I ask Baba for an explanation, I receive among other things the following answer:

Question: Baba, that feeling of bliss on the left side and pain on the right side, it feels like some sort of fight.

Baba: That's exactly what it is. It is the Kurukshetra. The heart is the Kurukshetra, the battlefield of contradictory forces. Enter into the fight and become the conquerer.

Q: But how do I enter into the fight?

B: By not running away from it.

Q: Do you mean that I must accept that this pain exists side by side with this feeling of joy?

B: Yes.

At one moment Baba lets me know that God and man are one. That there is no difference between us and Him. That it is important for us to know this.

Q: But I don't know what to do with this knowledge, and when that is so, why do I feel that pain then? I feel pain and still I am equal to God, one with God?

B: Do you think that I don't feel any pain? All your pain is my pain.

Q: Is the pain I feel also the pain of the world?

B: Pain belongs to existence. Pain and joy are one, split in two by life on earth.

172

Q: Is that why I feel so much bliss on one side—my heart—and pain on the other side?

B: Yes.

Q: They can exist side by side?

B: They exist side by side.

Q: But You have often said in Your discourses that joy and sorrow follow each other during our life on earth.

B: That is so in duality. In unity they exist side by side. Look at me. I experience all your pain and I am always full of Ananda.

Q: So, the pain I feel at my right side is the pain of the world?

B: No, it is your pain. Your coping with the situation in which you find yourself. It exists nevertheless at the same time as your bliss. There is no difference. One is not different from the other.

Q: Still, I would rather experience bliss than pain.

B: That is human thinking, not divine.

Q: I understand. Jesus took pain upon Himself of his own free will. He did not choose a blissful existence.

B: Jesus experienced bliss and pain as one.

Q: But still, He knew his moments of despair. Didn't He say, "Father, if thou be willing, remove this cup from me; nevertheless not my will, but thine, be done" (Luke 22:41) and also, "My God, my God why hast thou forsaken me" (Mark 15:34).

-no answer

Q: How is that, Baba?

B: By intensively experiencing this pain, He identified himself with humanity or rather humanity could identify with Him. That was His great sacrifice. He gave up Ananda of his own free will. He accepted the shadow-side of duality. The drama was enacted in Him, in the heart. It was enacted in three days, whereas people need many, many lives for it.

Q: So, in a human being it is first either Ananda or pain - often more pain than Ananda - and then Ananda gets the upper hand, but ultimately pain and Ananda exist simultaneously?

173

B: That's how it is.

Q: Is that peace of mind?

B: The acceptance of it is peace of mind.

Q: At one time You said that peace of mind is much more wonderful than bliss. But surely this simultaneous feeling of inner peace and pain isn't more wonderful than bliss?

B: It is. It makes you one with your fellow human beings. It raises you above the ego.

Q: You mean that living in bliss still implies ego?

B: It certainly does. You live in bliss and the world lives in pain? How can that be? Live in bliss and pain simultaneously, then you are truly one with the world.

Q: Yes, the world also lives in bliss and pain simultaneously. In some places peace, beauty and happiness prevail and in other places a war is going on.

B: You start to understand it.

Q: And we are a reflection of the world, so both also are prevalent in us?

B: Yes, and they do so at the same moment. The person who searches experiences pain and happiness as two successive states of being. The person who has found - who has knowledge - knows that both exist simultaneously.

Q: And one experiences them physically?

B: That can happen to make clear to you how it is possible, how it is a reality.

Q: And when one does not experience it physically?

B: Then one knows and is aware of the essence of the world.

Q: But don't we have to go beyond suffering, conquer suffering?

B: To let pain and happiness exist simultaneously is the victory over suffering.

Q: It does not mean enjoying pain, I think.

B: No, it has nothing to do with that. It has to do with recognizing the world in yourself. Knowing that you stand as symbol for the world. You ARE, which implies that you are as the world is.

Q: But one can hardly say this to someone who suffers.

B: No, that is useless. Such a person is taking part in suffering, not in the bliss of Ananda.

Q: I have the feeling that You want to let me know that it has to do with something very serious, with the earnestness of being, but I cannot put it into words very well.

B: It is a secret that only few people know. The time has come to reveal it.

Q: What is the secret then, that suffering and joy are one?

B: No, that suffering and joy can exist simultaneously and can be transcended that way. The person who lets both exist in himself and is impartial therein, who experiences suffering as part of bliss and bliss as part of suffering, this person co-operates in making the world whole.

Q: What does "whole" mean then?

B: "Whole" means: healed, stripped of duality. Made one in one continuous state of BEING, not interrupted by periods of suffering alternated with periods of bliss.

Q: Was the Buddha an example of this?

B: Yes.

Q: But wasn't Buddha in a continuous state of bliss?

B: With equal truth it can be said that Buddha was in a continuous state of pain. Suffering was conquered by accepting it. Bliss and suffering existed simultaneously, there was no difference.

49

BEING SURE

13 May 1996

Question: Baba, do You want me to write?

Baba: Yes.

Q: About what, Baba? (My heart feels softly glowing and loving, a sign that He is with me, but I do not get an answer. Well, actually I don't have any questions, I would like to write, but maybe that is only because it has been such a long time)

B: No, that is not the case.

Q: What is it then, Baba?

B: Open yourself to me and you will receive the answer.

Q: What do You want me to write about?

B: About being certain.

Q: Being certain of what?

B: The Self is certain. You must learn to follow the Self and to be certain.

Q: To be certain of what I want?

B: Just being certain, being firmly anchored in being certain of yourself.

Q: I am not certain of myself then?

B: No, there is still a part that doubts.

Q: Yes, that is true, Baba, this is really a struggle for me.

(I became aware of this after I had watched a TV programme sent out by the Dutch Evangelical Broadcasting Company a little while ago. In it Baba was ridiculed and Jesus was glorified at the expense of Baba. Due to the cunning and misleading manner in which it was presented, I was - though only for a short while-led to doubt, even though I realised at the same time that that was not at all what I wanted; I wanted to be so certain of Baba, that such a thing could not upset me in the least, not even for a short while).

B: That is what I mean by being certain.

Q: You mean being certain that You are who You are?

B: Yes.

Q: Yes, I would like to know this with much more certainty, with an unfailing faith. Why is wanting this not sufficient?

B: Wanting it is a start. However, wanting to have faith in God is not the same as having faith in God.

Q: No, I realize that. But how do I go from one to the other?

-No answer

Q: Why don't You answer, Baba?

B: There is no recipe for it. It involves feeling your way through life in full surrender to God. Abandoning yourself completely to Him and being steadfast in the knowledge that everything that happens is for your own good. Taking that as a starting point. Never doubting that, no matter what happens.

Q: And that is the same as not doubting God?

B: Of course, God is the one who has laid down your course.

Q: For everyone?

B: For everyone.

Q: So, accepting cheerfully what happens to you is the same as not doubting God; is, as it were, the way to fight doubt?

B: Yes.

Q: But when it so happens that I doubt, should I accept that cheerfully as well?

B: Yes, do not be ensnared by it, though. Live in the present, not in the memory of something that has happened. Go on and let yourself be carried along by the stream of events. Develop in that way an unfailing faith without any doubts.

Q: So, from now on, when I have a small doubt, like "Oh, what if they are right," as in the case of the TV programme, I accept that cheerfully in the manner of "this doubt has been given to me by God (Baba), thank You, God (Baba)." And then I go on with my life, with whatever is happening at that moment. And that I also accept cheerfully again.

B: Yes.

Q: I do not have to worry about it?

B: That's right.

Q: But isn't it the intention that we dedicate everything to You?

B: The one does not exclude the other.

Q: But at the moment I doubt You, I can hardly dedicate it to You, can I?

B: You can dedicate it to God.

Q: Yes, and He is You, so everything is all right.

B: Now do you see it?

Q: Yes, thank You Baba, it is all very simple really.

50
FORM AND FORMLESSNESS

28 June 1996

During my meditation two days ago I experienced something special. It was as if Baba spoke through me and said, "I am total, I am parameter". I looked up the word "parameter" in the Longman Dictionary and I found as an explanation something like: "limits within which something takes place". Since Baba first said, "I am total", I think that therefore the "limits within which something takes place" are in His case the utmost limits of the universe.

Question: Is that correct, Baba?

Baba: The utmost limits of the universe have been made continuous by me.

Q: What do You mean by that, Baba?

B: Transience has made place for perpetuity and its limits extend over the cosmos.

Q: You mean that if one reaches the limits of the cosmos, one goes beyond time?

B: That's correct.

Q: But we can never get there, can we?

B: Not in matter, but we can in the mind.

Q: We can think that we have arrived at the utmost limit of the universe, is that what You mean?

B: We are there the moment we think it.

Q: And have we gone beyond time then?

B: That is the way to go beyond time.

Q: So, this has to take place in our minds, in our thoughts?

B: Nothing is obligatory, but that is the way.

Q: But I cannot fathom how I can think of the limit of the cosmos, I cannot imagine anything then.

B: Not imagining anything is the same as imagining everything. The limit is the Void, which is All.

Q: What do You mean by "All" then?

B: The totality of existence.

Q: So, when You say, "I am total, I am parameter", You indicate that the totality includes at the same time the limit of all that is?

B: The totality *is* the limit of all that is.

Q: I want to look it up in the English dictionary once more.

B: Go ahead.

Q: The exact explanation of "parameter" is: "Any of the established limits within which something must operate".

B: Do you see it now? The established limits are those of the whole cosmos. Within it totality takes place. I am the limit of the event and the event itself.

Q: You are, as it were, the circumference of the circle ànd its contents?

B: That's right.

Q: And the circumference is the Void and the contents are all?

B: Equally one can say: the contents are nothing and the circumference is all.

Q: But the contents are - let me put it this way - life on earth, creation, and the circumference is God, or is that not so?

B: No, it is not as simple as that. Contents and circumference merge. It is the same as form and formlessness.

Q: You mean everything has a form, but still it is the Atma - the formlessness - that sustains us?

B: Yes, that is correct.

Q: But I can't grasp it, Baba.

B: It is not meant to be grasped.

Q: What is the meaning then?

B: It is meant to be experienced. To give the formless the upper hand. To let the formless reign over the form and not the other way around.

Q: Is that what we do, do we let the form reign over the formless?

B: Yes, people attach so much value to the form that they miss the formless principle, the principle that creates, preserves and destroys.

Q: You mean Brahma, Vishnu, Shiva?

B: Yes.

Q: And that is one?

B: Yes.

Q: What about the form then?

B: The form is a manifestation of the formless and not the other way around.

Q: Do we people often think that it is the other way around?

B: The individual who is trapped in the illusion of the form recognizes no reality other than that of the form.

Q: You mean life on earth?

B: Life in all its nuances.

Q: But still, You have said that life on earth is perfect. Life in the form.

B: The one does not exclude the other.

Q: What do You mean?

B: The formless - Atma - which creates every form, creates perfection out of perfection. The perfect EXISTENCE in all its forms.

Q: But if the form is perfect, isn't it logical then that we get trapped in it?

B: Here you touch the heart of the matter: as soon as you get trapped in the form, the latter stops being perfect. It moves away, as it were, it withdraws and what is left is appearance which expresses itself in pain and suffering.

Q: Difficult, Baba!

B: No, do not get attached, do not get trapped in the form. Realise that the form is never permanent, that it is created by the permanent which is formless.

Q: That is the parameter?

B: That is the parameter of the totality. The confusion came about because man began to put the form on a pedestal and forgot the formless principle, from which everything originated. It is essential to let this formless principle reverberate again in all we do.

Q: We are not allowed to enjoy the form?

B: Enjoy as much as you like. Be happy. However, enjoy the Self, God who has made all this for you. Enjoy existence by surrendering to the formless.

Q: But how do I do that, Baba?

B: Let God, the formless aspect of God, run your life. Allow Him to guide you. Expect nothing, ask nothing, let Him be. He lives in you. You are Him, open yourself thereto.

Q: Does that mean just going on with things as I have always done, or should I completely change over?

B: No, go on but be steadfast. If the Self in you decides, if it is God, the formless principle, who acts in you, nothing can go wrong. Be convinced of that. Do not doubt the Self, therefore do not doubt yourself.

Q: But what if I make mistakes?

B: If you let the Self work in you, you cannot make mistakes, that is impossible. The form surrenders to you in that case and not the other way around. That is the way to enjoy existence.

Q: Yes, then we see how beautifully it all ties up. Sometimes I can really look in admiration and wonder at for instance the flowers in the garden. Now the roses come out again. How is it possible? What a great miracle! Thank you for so much beauty. I know that all is temporary, but still this beauty returns year after year.

B: That will also pass one time; however, the wonder is essential, that is what remains. Wonder and admiration. These are timeless emotions which attach themselves to a temporary form, but which in themselves are timeless.

Q: So, the feeling of wonder comes close to the Atma?

B: Yes.

Q: Does the Atma wonder then?

B: The Atma IS. It is the individual, who starts to grasp something of creation, who cannot but stand in wonder.

Q: To stand in wonder and to admire are very closely related then?

B: They are equal to one another. Admiration implies wonder and vice versa.

Q: I love You, Baba and I wonder each time again at how simple and blissful it is to know You, but I want more. I want You with me. I want to know why I have been created, why we have been created. What the use is of this all, even though You say that there is no use, that it is as it is. I want there to be more than this. Even this blissful feeling in my heart. But how and what that more is... ? Maybe it is to see your appearance here in the room. But then again, if that is also only temporary, it isn't really what I want either. I would like the temporary and the timeless to become one, is that possible Baba?

B: That is the parameter of totality.

Q: There is a thinking "I", who gets up, does things, goes shopping, cooks, works behind the computer, but is that me, Baba, or is that the form?

B: It isn't you and it is you. It could be you, really BE you, if you consciously let the Atma guide your actions. If you forgo what you think you want and let the things that must happen take place without passing judgement.

Q: But it seems to me that I would become some kind of robot then.

B: Why?

Q: A will-less person who lets himself be guided will-lessly.

B: If it is God who guides you, there is nothing wrong with that. There is nothing will-less to it. God's will in you is the supreme will. You would certainly not go through life as will-less, but as extremely powerful and energetic. Radiant with Godliness is he who subordinates his will to God's will. Who subordinates his form to the formless. Who subordinates the transient to what is unchangeable.

Q: Yes, the bliss (Ananda) in my heart has felt the same for years. The strength and frequency may differ, but the feeling is one and the same. Is that what You mean?

B: Bliss is unchangeable. From bliss you live, what you feel is bliss, the blissfulness of existence. That blissfulness is unchangeable. It can be experienced to a greater or lesser extent, however.

Q: And if we don't feel it, it is there all the same?

B: Of course, that is the essence of unchangeability.

Q: Also when we are dead?

B: Yes, then also. Bliss is permanent. Sometimes you experience it, at other times you don't. That doesn't alter the unchangeable character of bliss.

Q: As if it exists by itself?

B: It exists by itself.

Q: Actually I - my form - do not really exist, for I change constantly and eventually I will die, but this bliss will remain eternally and is there for everyone?

B: Yes.

Q: I am starting to grasp it a little. And that bliss is God?

B: Yes.

Q: Or Atma?

B: Atma as well.

Q: But don't we also have to go beyond bliss. We should also go beyond the Anandamaya Kosa, shouldn't we?

B: That simply means that it should not become an end in itself. You don't live to experience bliss. You live to become one with God and the closer you get to your goal, the more God's blissfulness will be felt. Do not be ensnared by it, though. Do not think that the goal is that blissfulness. The goal is God. He is blissfulness and goes beyond blissfulness.

Q: How then?

B: God is the all. You are the all. Be satisfied only when you have reached God. When you have become God. Then everything will be your share.

Q: But isn't it true that I don't want anything anymore then?

B: You don't want anything anymore then and therefore everything will be your share.

Q: Can one experience this state by, for example, going out of the body?

B: That is possible, but not necessary. You can experience this state by living fully consciously with God; with God, through God and for God.

Q: Yes Baba, the happiness this certainty gives is more wonderful than bliss; I experienced it once and I want to revert to it. "God is always with me" sang through me and was a reality. It was self-evident. Now, when I only think of it, when I don't experience it as I did then, it takes an effort which I don't feel like, or should I try to re-experience that state by means of a thought-process?

B: No, not by way of thinking. God is with you when you are good, when you think good, when you act good. His approval expresses itself in your knowing that He is with you, in your experiencing His omnipresence.

Q: As self-evidently as when Jesus said, "My Father and I are one" and also, "It is not I, but my Father who works in me"?

B: Yes, that self-evidently.

51
WE ARE GOD

8 July 1996
In Baba's ashram in Puttaparthi again

Question: Baba, actually I am still very often insecure and feeling very insignificant, notably about the teachings. It is often only in retrospect that I realize that they are valuable, but at the moment itself - like now, for instance - I would like to obtain more from You, more clarity.

Baba: You will get it.

Q: But when?

B: Wait. Exercising patience is a good thing. You must learn to overcome that insecurity. Know that you are God, equal to me. Do not be diffident about it.

Q: But isn't that "spiritual pride", something very haughty?

B: No, this can be known in all humility. God knows that He is God and He is humility itself. Do not be afraid of being worth nothing. Let that fear come to the fore and conquer it.

Q: But I could conquer it much more easily if You would let me experience or show me more of Yourself.

B: No, that would only be temporal, immediately after you would fall back again into insecurity. It would be a single - or repeated - event in your life, at which you would look back with love, attention and great interest.

Q: But wouldn't I also learn from it?

B: Certainly, but you can't get self-confidence from it.

Q: Why do we people have to take such pains to really be aware that we are God?

B: The ego pulls man down.

Q: But isn't it fantastic for the ego to know that it is God?

B: No, the ego can never realize or experience this. The ego is earth-bound and pulls man downward. Godliness is beyond the comprehension of the ego. That is the great fight. The ego fights against your Godliness. You yourself will have to decide which is going to win.

Q: But how?

B: Lose your ego, become humble.

Q: Oh Baba, how do I do that? I feel far from Godly, I still have so many faults.

B: Work on them. Face your faults. Do not disguise them and don't make things nicer than they are. Only when a person really dares to face up to his faults, can he work on solving them.

52
THE CROWN-CHAKRA

9 July 1996
Waiting for Baba, after morning-darshan

Question: I feel rather unsettled, Baba. I would like to correspond with You, but I don't know if that is what You want.

Baba: I want it, write about love.

Q: But You have already said such beautiful things about love, what could be added to it?

B: Love is the willingness to make sacrifices for other people. Love is sacrificing oneself for the benefit of others.

Q: But isn't it a fact that You want us to stand up for ourselves, Baba?

B: Love is standing up for yourself and at the same time sacrificing yourself for others. The former does not exclude the latter, never.

Q: But isn't it a fact that people who always sacrifice themselves for others often break down? And then they are of no use to anyone anymore.

B: When your love expands itself to others, to the Self in others, which is your Self as well, when you love the Self, whether it has taken the form of another person or your form, you exercise true love. The Self in you is the Self in the other person, there is no difference.

Q: So, actually I myself, my lower self that is, am also the other person.

B: Yes, the lower self, your lower self, is as much the other person as other people are where it concerns their lower selves.

Q: So, then I should look at myself as if I were looking at another person?

B: Yes.

Q: But still, it is with my own body that I look.

B: That is only partly true. The Atma is everything and everywhere and when you perceive from the Atma, it is both in you and outside you. Picture the Atma as being outside you, then it will be easier for you to look from the Atma at yourself.

Q: Should I do the same when I look at others?

B: The view will be better, the insights clearer, the recognition greater, if you try to place the Atma outside of you and look from there.

Q: May I place it above my head? I already experienced once that my consciousness was situated there.

B: Above the crown-chakra is the place where the Atma is optimally situated when it has formed itself into a person. Experience the world, yourself included, from that place, and love will be your share.

Q: Love for me or love from me to others?

B: Both, there is no difference after all! You look then from love at love, at yourself as the other and at the other as yourself.

Q: I just tried to look that way, Baba, but I find it difficult. It does not feel true.

B: It requires exercise. Go on with it, daily, until it has become second nature.

Q: What I do is I place, as it were, my consciouness above my head?

B: Yes.

Q: And what about my heart then?

B: The heart is the place from which love wells up. There is a connection between the heart and the crown. The stream ought to go from the heart to the crown.

Q: And back again?

B: That isn't necessary. The heart is filled with divine love, the stream is eternal.

53

EMOTIONS

12 July 1996
At the temple-compound, after morning-darshan

I feel peaceful and quiet. I experience my mind as a motionless, transparent lake. That should be wonderful, but I don't find it wonderful. I want visions and dreams and emotions and attention. I think I've not yet attained the level of this peaceful nothingness. It does feel pleasant and agreeable, but too detached. I would like it to be Baba who gives me this peace, I don't want it to stem from myself. Intellectually I understand that what I am saying is far from correct, for nothing would be better than that this peaceful feeling would stem from myself, that would mean that He and I are one; but I am still at the stage that I want Him as the Other. That is probably due to the fact that I am not yet used to this stage of BEING.

Question: Is that so, Baba, have I understood it more or less correctly?

Baba: Yes.

Q: But I would rather experience emotions. This quiet, transparent nothingness is agreeable but not exciting. Sorrow, as I felt yesterday, because I didn't get line 1, which I could have had if I hadn't changed lines, seems preferable. At least that is recognisable. This feeling I cannot compare to anything. And that in the presence of God! Here I am sitting, cool and unaffected. I find it so strange. Then again it is more internal than external. Externally I do feel ill at ease with all kinds of small inconveniences like the heat, the cramped space, the occasional power failure, my roommate who is ill, etc. But when You pass by, I seem unmoved, blank. I don't want that, Baba.

B: It is good the way it is.

Q: But why?

B: Eventually that is the state of BEING you should reach. Beyond emotions. Emotions are addictions acquired in many, many lives. Emotions are addictive and keep the addiction going at the same time, just like drugs.

Q: But to be emotionless seems so unfeeling.

B: Emotionless feeling is true compassion. Offering comfort without emotion but with compassion is the best comfort there is.

Q: So, compassion is not an emotion?

B: No, it has nothing to do with emotion. It is timeless. It is love.

Q: But isn't love an emotion then?

B: Love is timeless as well, has nothing to do with emotion, with a habit-forming feeling. Do not be misled about this. Many people commit this mistake. Compassion is timeless, eternal. Emotions are defined by place and culture.

Q: I don't understand, Baba. Or do You mean, to give an example, that in the Arab culture people are loudly sobbing at funerals, whereas in the West sorrow is professed somewhat less openly?

B: Yes.

Q: But both cultures eventually know the feeling of sorrow due to loss, don't they?

B: The feeling of sorrow is very different from one culture to the other and is also differently coped with.

Q: Does this hold true also for parental love?

B: Mother-love tends toward the timeless, beyond emotions. Father-love is defined by culture.

Q: That is not very nice for all those fathers.

B: Why not? There is nothing wrong with that. Emotions belong to daily life. However, recognize them for what they are.

Q: So, mother-love is not an emotion.

B: Ideally it is not. However, it is also often defined by culture and then it is of a lower quality. As long as a person does not know any better, this is what happens.

Q: I cannot at all picture a world in which everyone is cool and emotionless.

B: It will never be that way, people are in different stages of their development. At the same time we are not speaking here about things that are superficially recognisable. What is recognisable to us is functioning in the world, doing the task which is at hand.

Q: Yes, that I understand and then for example a baker who does his work well, without emotions, is of more use to me than an emotional baker.

B: Exactly.

Q: So, when we do our work well and carefully, society will not present itself to us as a detached, emotionless world?

B: That's the way is is. That's what it is all about. Do your work fully dedicated, with a willingness to sacrifice. Place yourself in the service of other people. The more unmoved by emotions you do this, the more effective your work for others.

Q: It is starting to dawn on me, but I don't really understand this condition yet. For when I apply it to myself, I could ask myself, "what is 'doing my work as well as possible'? Couldn't it be that there is ego behind just that? That you do it to gain recognition?"

B: In that case you let yourself be led by emotions again. Wanting to be recognized is an emotion, a very deeply rooted one, which stems from insecurity. You are not guided by compassion then, being disinterestedly available for your fellow-human beings.

Q: Is that what compassion is?

B: Yes.

Q: Then actually we should put every emotion to the test of compassion: is what I am doing of service to others?

B: Every act should be put to that test. When emotions have the upper hand in such a case, you should consult yourself and mark time. Look at yourself, recognize it and try to introduce a change in it.

Q: This goes for every emotion?

B: Yes.

Q: Also for anger, jealousy, envy, etc.?

B: Of course. If work is done from one of these motives, you may as well not do it.

Q: But in the western world the competitive drive is seen as the highest good.

B: It isn't and it will never be. Compassion for others should be the incentive of any work, whatever it is.

Q: Any work is important?

B: No work can exist by itself.

Q: Baba, You are now in the interview room with some Indian gentlemen and I am here corresponding with You. Is this what is called truth?

B: Yes.

Q: This is how I can come to an understanding of it: it is not You - Your physical form - who corresponds with me, but my inner Baba. You are occupied with quite other things. (The very moment I write this, my heart starts glowing softly; for me this is a sign that it must be true, that He is with me and that He wants to make this clear to me. And - back in Holland, half a year later - at the exact moment when I have come to this point in typing out the text, that loving warmth settles again in my heart, as an extra confirmation).

B: My work is for all things and all people, always. There is no difference. I work in, for and through everyone. I am not limited to my physical body. I work for everything and everyone for sheer compassion. I reflect on the previous, especially on what He said about emotions, then I ask:

Q: But this glowing heart, this bliss, Ananda, isn't that something which is felt?

B: It is not a feeling in the sense of an emotion. It is timeless and unchangeable, not defined by culture.

Q: So, if what we feel is timeless, unchangeable, not defined by culture, it is not an emotion?

B: That's what it comes down to.

Q: Like love?

B: Spiritual love most certainly. Mother-love comes close to the ideal. The rest is interwoven with emotions and therefore not pure love, which is unchangeable and not defined by culture.

Q: Yes, I understand. The love a man and a woman feel for each other is experienced very differently in different countries and also in different times.

B: Love as an emotion is functional, but it is not the universal, spiritual love from which everything originated, to which everything will return and of which man on earth is the manifestation. As soon as he has become conscious of this, the emotions will withdraw one by one and their place will be taken up by the unchangeable feeling of equanimity, of compassion and love.

O: And that is a blank feeling, as if there is a motionless lake inside oneself?

B: If the lake is transparent, this is correct. If the lake is troubled, you have landed in apathy, which, just like emotions, is not good.

Q: Could one compare emotions with Rajas, apathy with Tamas, and what You speak about, compassion, with Satwa?

B: Yes.

Q: So, actually you spoke about the three Gunas?

B: About two of them. Tamas has not been broached, that will come at another time.

54
THE INNER SAI

14 July 1996
At the temple-compound, after morning-darshan

Baba is in the interview room, but my Baba is in my heart, with me and around me. That is the source from which I draw. Yesterday this suddenly became clear to me and today, when I think it over, I am aware that this is how it really is. Baba here, in the form, is a symbol of it, but the real Baba is in my heart.

Question: Is this the way it is, Baba?

Baba: Yes, that's the way it is and that's how it should be experienced by everyone.

Q: But when You appear on earth in a form, isn't it logical then that people take Your form for the real Baba?

B: My form is a reflection of the Sai-consciousness, the God-consciousness in every human being. But as long as man is not aware of this, as long as he tries to find this in outer manifestations, he needs the form. The form, however, including my form, is an illusion. The form is subject to change and is impermanent, therefore it cannot be truth. Truth is the Sai-consciousness in every being.

Q: But You are truth, aren't You? Your name is Truth!

B: I am truth in the sense that I stand as a symbol for the Sai-consciousness which is true. My form has adopted the name Truth, my essence IS truth.

Q: But it is in the form that You look at people and transform them.

B: The transformation goes from heart to heart. Looking at things is again one of those externals which man yearns for, because he cannot grasp the unchangeable truth, the inner Sai-consciousness. They are not only the people here in Prashanti Nilayam who are seen by God. God's view is not limited by his physical eyes. Whoever thinks so is taking the wrong path.

Q: But then it isn't necessary at all that people come here.

B: As said before: Optimally it isn't necessary. Man, however, has became so caught up in the world of phenomena that he wants to experience even God as a phenomcnon. As long as he hasn't done so, complete belief is impossible for him.

Q: So, in that respect it is important that people come here.

B: The individual who is totally focused on God, who experiences God in himself, has no need to come here.

Q: But they do come?

B: Some do, in honour of my physical form.

Q: But then again, didn't the Gopis also want your physical form?

B: The Gopis represent the individual who yearns for God, who intensely longs for God, who is focused one-pointedly on experiencing God. They do not represent the individual who has realised God and has gone beyond the form.

Q: So, the people who come to You in the ashram can be compared to the Gopis?

B: Most of them, not all. Not everyone comes here because of an intensive feeling of yearning. There are those who are merely curious and there are those who want to catch me in falsehood.

Q: But You love them all equally?

B: My children who err are equally dear to me. They are the ones who need to be corrected. Just as a mother pays more attention to the difficult child, I pay more attention to the correction process of those who err. Divine love is inclusive of everything and everyone, you know that.

Q: Sometimes I think that all this correspondence with You is only to make things clear to myself and to get them straight, and that that is all it is.

B: When you get things straight for yourself, it is God in you who does so. It is the Sai-consciousness that speaks.

Q: But what I don't understand is how Your physical form can also be aware of this.

B: That is the mystery of God which is beyond man's comprehension.God experiences Himself in everything, in every blade of grass, in every animal, in every part of nature and above all in every human being. There is no difference between the Sai-consciousness of one individual and another and the totality of all those consciousnesses has centered itself in my physical form; centered and concentrated. The Sai-consciousness, however, is infinitely more comprehensive than what man, with his perishable body, percieves when he looks at me.

Q: You said once that we created You as well as You created us.

B: The intense yearning after God of sages and God-seekers has made this triple incarnation come about. In that respect you could say that man has created me. This approach is not fully correct, though. However, it is true that, as there is no difference between God and man, man separated himself from himself into God as much as God separated Himself from Himself into Creation.

Q: Do You mean man, or Creation in its totality?

B: I mean Creation with man as the culmination of Creation. Man is the last evolution-form of Creation in the process of returning consciously to the Creator.

Q: We, as Creation, were unaware, didn't know about Your existence, and now, as man, we become aware? Is it then also true that God was first unaware and became aware through our existence, through the existence of Creation?

B: That is partly true; however, you pass over the phenomenon of time. You don't take that into account. Time is also part of Creation. God is timeless. Creation is defined by time. That which is without time has always been aware of itself.

Q: But was it also aware of Creation?

B: Timelessness knows Creation as one and undivided. Present, past and future are one. God, separated from Himself, and God, one in Himself, is not a contradiction. This is where man's comprehension, which is bound to time, fails.

Q: So, I don't need to pursue this subject, Baba?

B: You could ask who created time.

Q: You did, didn't You?

B: Since in timelessness Creator and Creation are one, with equal right can be said that Creation created timelessness.

Q: So, God made Creation come about and then Creation created time?

B: Yes, that is evident when you regard the workings of time in the cosmos.

Q: And at the same time timelessness existed?

B: At the same time timelessness <u>exists</u>, that also is evident when you regard the workings of time in the cosmos.

Q: The way I can comprehend it is: it appears that when we look at stars and galaxies, we actually look at something that took place a long time ago. So, we look back in time. I have read that when we come to the outer boundaries of the cosmos, Creation takes place there. Is that what You mean?

B: Yes, that approaches it. The cosmos, however, is limitless, knows no boundaries. Creation, though, takes place at this moment and is completed at this moment. Studying the cosmos helps to come to some understanding of it. Studying the Self, the Atma, will yield more understanding, though. Because the Self equals Creation and Creator. In the Self Sai-consciousness can express itself and all knowledge is made known.

After some time

Q: Baba, I still feel quiet and calm inside like a transparent lake. Everything seems to be clear, without words, so that is good?

B: Yes.

Q: But externally I am not at all that placid, I can hardly concentrate anymore during meditation.

B: Nor is there any need for that. Your writing is meditation.

Q: And fortunately the weather is rather cool now, for I find the heat here unbearable.

B: I gave you that coolness.

Q: I know that, but surely I am not like a transparent lake then?

B: The point is the inner life. As a manifestation in the world, as a human phenomenon you are subject to all man has to cope with.

Q: But what about such people as Yogis and Saddhus, don't they transcend those things?

B: Choose the way of moderation. Follow the example of the Buddha. You need not practice abnegation and corporal chastisement. Give the body what is due to the body, no more and no less.

Q: And if it feels incommoded?

B: Do something about it; and only when that is not possible, try reaching the Atma with the mind to make yourself free from the body. This only as a last resource. When the body requires food and food is available, feed it. When the body requires liquid and liquid is available, refresh it. Beware of excess, however. Know your limits. Also know the limits of your body. Know what is good for you and what isn't. Do not indulge in anything. Keep the body healthy by listening to your body. Self-denial and chastisement are not required; only in exceptional cases, which have to do with Karma. Most people, however, who choose the way of abnegation, choose the wrong way. Look at nature, nature does not deprive itself of anything.

Q: Then what about fasting?

B: Fasting is good for a body that has too many toxins in it. Never too long, however.

Q: So, we should eat pure, Satwic food and we need not practice abnegation like a kind of hermit.

B: That's correct.

55
THE SAI-CONSCIOUSNESS

15 July 1996
At the temple-compound, between darshan and bhajans

Question: You want me to write, Baba?

Baba: Yes.

Q: I don't have any questions.

B: You have many.

Q: Yes, that's true, Baba. Should I accept the function that is offered to me? Is that beneficial to my progress or will it only make my ego grow?

-No answer

Q: Why don't You answer?

B: It is your own choice.

Q: But I would like to make progress on the spiritual path and what if this keeps me from it?

B: That is also your choice.

Q: But surely You protect Your devotees from making mistakes?

B: I intervene when things threaten to go completely wrong, but not beforehand.

Q: Why not?

B: Man has free will.

Q: But what if he misuses this?

B: Again, only when things become life-threatening, I intervene.

Q: But what if I would fall behind on the spiritual ladder?

B: That is also your own choice.

Q: But I don't know if for instance this function will make me fall behind or not.

B: If you carry it out with a pure heart, without putting your ego to the fore, if you make yourself available as a servant of all, you will not fall behind.

Q: But I have no idea if I am able to do so.

B: Then don't accept the function.

Meanwhile my heart has started glowing again, first softly and then more and more. I keep finding it strange, Baba is occupied in the interview room and here outside I am communicating with Him.

Q: Is it You, Baba, in the interview room who is communicating with me, or am I communicating with that burning glow in my heart?

B: There is no difference.

Q: Yes, I have come to understand that now. Still, it is the Baba within who pays attention to me and not You.

B: I am the motivator of the Baba within.

Q: But Your form is perishable. The Baba within me is permanent.

B: My form is perishable because I willed it so. My essence isn't. It is the Sai-consciousness, the Sai-esssence that is the motivator of everything and everyone. This takes place whether I am in the form on earth or not.

Q: But now that You are here in the form, is it Your form that motivates things?

B: No, it is still the Sai-essence, my essence, that motivates all things and that is as much your essence. Only I am aware of it and you are not; aware of it to the depths of my physical structure. I am aware of each atom of my body and it is through my will that this body originated and is kept together as a body. The Sai-consciousness, my consciousness, comprises the whole cosmos, however.

Q: And is it that consciousness which makes use of me as a writer?

B: The Sai-consciousness settled in your vehicle, because your vehicle has writing potential.

Q: But what if I don't use it?

B: Many lives are needed to stimulate the potential in man to its optimal use. What is not accomplished in this life, will be completed in another.

Q: But then I am another personality again.

B: Yes.

Q: Then what has remained the same?

B: The amount of accumulated consciousness. That never gets lost, wherever you incarnate.

Q: So, if I give up now, I will find myself at this level of consciousness in a next life?

B: Yes.

Q: Right away?

B: That depends on other Karmic involvements. How much has still to be set right? That is what is worked on in an incarnation. Only when these things have been worked out, does the progressive accumulation of consciousness get a chance to develop any further.

Q: So, we can only work on our Sai-consciousness, if a large part of our Karma has been worked out?

B: Yes.

Q: Each life anew?

B: Yes.

Q: But isn't it so that You take away Karma?

B: I take Karma away when the individual is open to my grace, when his consciousness is in tune with mine.

Q: Before that, You let him mess about?

B: If you want to call it that. It isn't messing about, though. All things that take place in a lifetime are valuable lessons to thus arrive at Sai-consciousness.

Q: Sai-consciousness is the same as God-consciousness?

B: That has been said already.

Q: All the same, I'd rather call it communicating with my Self, with Sai in me, for You in the interview room are now occupied with others.

B: Call it what you like. Go beyond the intellect. Do not try to explain it with the laws of worldly logic. Sai is in you and Sai is in the interview room. Sai is in everything and everyone.

Q: Is Sai also in Sai?

B: No, Sai is Sai.

Q: And man himself is also Sai but he doesn't know this?

B: Indeed.

Q: I want to grasp it. I want more. I want Your form, Baba.

B: Be content with what you have. The future is not yours to know. Have patience and confidence. Have faith.

Q: In myself or in You?

B: Is there a difference?

Q: I have faith in You, I do not have faith in myself.

B: You do not have faith in your lower self. When you have faith in me, you likewise have faith in your Self. Those two are not separable.

56
THE VALUE OF BEING

17 July 1996
At the temple-compound, after morning-darshan

Question: Baba, You want me to write?

Baba: Yes, write about the value of BEING.

Q: What is that?

B: BEING is valuable. BEING is life. BEING is happiness. BEING is bliss.

Q: But we don't always experience it that way.

B: Once you realize that this is true, you can also experience it as such.

Q: But isn't life very difficult and burdensome for quite a lot of people?

B: That is the value of BEING.

Q: So, that value need not always be positive?

B: BEING is always positive.

Q: All right, the value of BEING is positive, but what about those difficult lives then?

B: When you climb a mountain, you run into stumbling-blocks. You may even fall back some way. The road seems hard, the goal far, but eventually you will reach the top and then all of it was worth it. That is the value of BEING.

Q: Is BEING the top of that mountain then?

B: No, BEING is the whole process, from the moment you stand at the bottom of the mountain up to reaching the top.

Q: And beyond that?

B: Beyond it is unity with God.

Q: Why then that hard road to reach the top?

B: You chose for it yourself.

Q: Every person?

B: Yes, every person anew.

Q: But we don't know that anymore.

B: That is the dilemma, for which man himself also chose.

Q: For this not knowing?

B: For throwing himself in full confidence into the adventure without knowing why. Love is the motive. Love of BEING. Love for God who willed it so.

Q: What God wills must be good.

B: Yes, that's the faith you should cultivate. That's the whole point. Everything is good, because God wills it so. Experience everything as such, even the hardest path will be light then.

Q: God is my Father and He chooses a hard path for me? Why? Doesn't a father want things to go smoothly?

B: A father wants his child to go to school, don't you agree? What child would, in retrospect, blame his father for this? Still, for some children school-time can be very difficult and tough.

Q: So, life is some kind of school?

B: Yes, so it is.

Q: To become completely purified and to let go of our animal tendencies?

B: Yes.

Q: It seems logical. You say, though, that we choose the difficulties ourselves, but a child doesn't choose to go to school himself, does he?

B: Maybe not consciously, but his birth already defined his choice.

Q: So, he took birth consciously in a certain country with a certain family.

B: In most cases yes. Not always, though, as you have already been told.

Q: And then he lives with a certain family and again he doesn't know who he really is, and he thinks for instance, "I have to go to school, how annoying," but deep down he knows very well that it is for his own good?

B: Yes.

Q: So, I know very well that the fact that You don't give me an interview is for my own good?

B: Yes.

Q: But why, am I doing something wrong?

B: No, that's not it.

Q: I should learn to have faith that God knows best what is good for me and that "not getting an interview" is therefore good for me?

B: Yes.

Q: Even though I don't understand it, I should have confidence that it is good?

B: Yes and what's more, you should be glad with it. You should be glad with each situation that God gives you, always. Thanking God when things are easy, is easy enough, but thanking God, even when things are difficult, when they don't go the way you want, that is the lesson.

Q: Yes, seen in that light, my problems are simple enough. There are many things infinitely worse. And even then people should thank God?

B: Yes.

Q: But they aren't able to do so. Who is able to thank God when he finds himself in for instance an earthquake or a flood?

B: It is difficult, but it can be done. There are people who keep this equanimity under any circumstance.

Q: And when they don't, do You blame them?

B: God never blames anyone for anything. Man is predestined to be who he is, immersed in the situation in which he finds himself, and when that situation entails rebellion - even rebellion against God - it is a phase in which he finds himself. Happier however, is the person who praises God in all circumstances. In the long run it is not God who harms you, but you yourself.

Q: I get it, but it seems almost impossible to accomplish.

B: Start with not asking yourself, "why me?" Acceptance, praising God for what happens to you, will come in a later stage. Start with cheerfully accepting your lot.

Q: Is it contentment that You are talking about?

B: Yes, contentment under all circumstances.

57
INTERACTION

Question: Is a fully-realised person completely aware of the Sai-consciousness?

Baba: Yes, the Sai-consciousness is the motivator of his life. The Self and the Sai-consciousness have joined forces.

Q: Is that merging?

B: Yes, when it takes place optimally, that is what is called merging.

Q: Is such a person aware of this?

B: Not always. Man can think that I am the Other, whereas in essence I am him, whereas in essence he has reached me.

Q: Why is that so?

B: As long as a person lives on earth, he falls under earthly laws and he has to deal with interaction with his fellow-man. It is I who takes the place of his fellow-man and interaction with me takes the place of interaction with his fellow-man.

Q: So, he sees You as the Other, as someone different from himself?

B: He can't do otherwise as long as he is bound to the earth.

Q: Is that what You mean by interaction?

B: Yes, this interaction with me comes instead of merging with me. Even the person who has merged will, as long as he lives, experience this as communication with me and not as "being Me". This is not possible on earth. We are the other, there is no difference, but we experience diversity.

Q: Yes, I start to grasp it a little. Is that why it is impossible for us to understand unity, because we can never see another person as ourselves - literally as ourselves, I mean - even if we are realised?

B: Then also the other person remains "the other". Only, the other person can be experienced the same way as one experiences oneself then. This always takes time, however, and time is, as you know, closely linked to the earth. Time is linked to matter, just as much as the earth is. To adjust oneself to another person always requires time and therefore takes time. No matter how little that time may be.

Q: And the duration that such an adjustment requires, has to do with the degree of being realised?

B: No, with the nature of being realised.

Q: What do You mean by that?

B: There may be realised people on earth, who are not able to put themselves in somebody else's position.

Q: But how are they able to experience unity then?

B: They don't occupy themselves with that.

Q: What do You mean?

B: They experience the Self and that suffices.

Q: But isn't the Self in them and in the other person one then?

-No answer

Q: How is that?

B: They don't occupy themselves with it. This is an intellectual approach and on that level a realised person can withdraw himself therefrom.

Q: So, he keeps seeing another person as another person?

B: Again, he doesn't occupy himself with it.

Q: I don't understand, one has to deal with others, or not?

B: Yes, but this can be a natural process in which you don't occupy yourself with the question whether you and the other person are one or not.

Q: More as babies experience their mothers?

B: Yes, it can be compared to that.

Q: There is love then?

B: There is only love. A baby experiences his mother as undifferentiated from himself.

Q: But that stops, doesn't he slowly but surely become aware that they are not one?

B: Yes, and in the case of the realised person or the one who is getting there, the process is reversed. From the awareness of separation comes this stage of being undifferentiated, without this being a conscious thought-process.

Q: Can this also be experienced now and then as a kind of peak-experience, is it what we call a peak-experience?

B: That's how it is experienced by most seekers. Being continuously in this state of BEING is only given to a few.

Q: You just said, "There may be realised people on earth who are not able to put themselves in somebody else's position". Does this mean that there is also another type of realised person, who is able to completely identify himself with someone else?

B: Yes, there you say it as it is.

Q: Does that often happen?

B: That also only happens very rarely. That also may happen periodically in a human life, but to be continuously in this state of omniscience is also only given to a few.

Q: Is it important wanting to go consciously to one of these two states of BEING?

B: Important is wanting to let God work in you. The result of His work in you should be left to Him.

58
SELF-CONFIDENCE

10 September 1996

One of my cats had been missing for two nights and one day. When she was gone, I asked Baba during my meditation if He would please let her come back. I realised that I was sad about it. I thought "we don't know anything, we cannot see any further than the walls of the room in which we find ourselves; how then can we accept everything with equanimity?" I realised that I was still quite attached to things, far from being detached, the way Baba wants us to be. And then the thought passed my mind "So what, I am who I am! Yes, I am attached to things, and even worse, I like being attached. I like loving my pets. Of course someone else's pets are as dear, but these are mine, these are the ones I know. And I love my house. All right, it is His house, I got it from Him, but I am attached to it; "fortunately" - I am apt to say - I am attached to it and to many other things as well. And if that is bad, so be it!" Then it seemed as if Baba inwardly said:

Baba: That is being detached, accepting that you are attached.

Question: Can You explain that?

B: The process of attaching oneself is a process of many lives. It is an achievement which should not be given up light-heartedly.

Q: But don't You want us to be detached?

B: You should be able to leave everything behind the moment you are leaving the earth. Therefore it is important to know that everything is temporary. However, it is equally important to love what surrounds you.

Q: But when, as in the case of my cat, I couldn't let things be and what's more, I didn't want to let things be, how can that be good? Don't You want us to completely let go of everything?

B: I want you to leave everything to me. I want you to learn to have confidence that what happens is good, good for you and good for whoever you are worrying about.

Q: But such terrible things happen to people and animals!

B: Being detached means not worrying about all kinds of things that don't apply to the situation you are in. Trusting that it will end up all right. It is lack of trust that causes disasters. One can be attached and detached at the same time. Being detached does not mean that you shouldn't feel sad when something dear to you is taken away from you or seems to be taken away. Being detached means that you keep trusting that what happens is good, despite your sadness.

Q: So, I don't need, in a manner of speaking, to shout exultedly, "hurray, my cat is missing, that is what Baba wants." I can be sad, miss the cat enormously and at the same time trust that the outcome will be good, whatever it is.

B: Yes, that's what it comes down to.

Q: And I may ask You to help resolve the situation in which I find myself?

B: You may ask that any time. Place all your problems before me. Asking for a solution creates trust.

Q: But Baba, I became aware that there are still so many things that I am attached to, my house (Your house), my working situation, my living situation, the people I care for, my pets, BEING, yes, life itself. Now that I have got You in my life, life is so wonderful. I wouldn't want to be detached from it. I love life and everything it entails.

B: Loving existence is a great good. That is the attachment that we all have to experience. It is divine happiness to recognise all things created, to experience happiness in all things created. It is acceptance of the Self in all that is created, it is happiness because of the Self, your Self. That is the attachment to the earth, to the material world, for which you came to earth, life after life. That attachment is an achievement. It came from pure consciousness. It is pure consciousness.

Q: Do animals have it as well?

B: No, animals are who they are.

Q: But when they are in difficulties?

B: Then they will want to back away from them.

Q: But aren't they glad then when they are out of it?

B: They will be relieved, but this does not go via their consciousness but via their instinctive faculty. There is a difference.

Q: But doesn't the animal also know the feeling of being attached to the earth?

B: The animal is not aware of it, that is the difference. The awareness of being attached to, connected with, the earth is what entails great joy. It is a divine awareness.

Q: But how can that be reconciled with what You say about being detached?

B: When we have become optimally attached to existence, when we enjoy the pleasures of existence, only then are we fully detached. We stand above pain and sorrow then. You are happy to be alive, you begin to experience what it is to BE. BEING is knowing that one is connected with all things that ARE, with the whole of creation.

Q: And that may be experienced and felt as attachment to life?

B: That is surrendering oneself to life with complete trust and there is nothing wrong with it.

Q: And then when something happens that is sad, we may also surrender ourselves to sadness?

B: Yes, you may be sad, you may experience what it is to be sad. However, keep being confident that it is good to live.

Q: Is that being detached, feeling sadness and still being happy to live?

B: Yes.

Q: But I think that at a such moment - and of course the degree of calamity is relevant as well - one doesn't want to live at all.

B: Is that so?

Q: I don't know. I am only talking about my cat, but suppose one's child is missing that way, may not come back anymore, does one still want to go on living then as a parent?

B: Again, it is a matter of confidence. To what degree is that parent capable of trusting that it is God's will that has prevailed?

Q: But isn't that quite impossible in such a situation?

B: Nothing is impossible.

Q: But how can God want a child to be brutally mistreated?

B: Trusting that it is good, is not to say that God condones these things happening. It is to say that God is present and alleviates sorrow and pain. God is the great surgeon, who does not let his children suffer in vain. And who makes all things light. Holding on to that confidence in the most terrible of circumstances that may befall you and those dear to you, will help you, always.

Q: And that is being detached?

B: That has to do with it.

After some time

Q: I have this feeling that as long as I live on earth, I have a right to enjoy what the earth has to offer.

B: You have that right, but the enjoyment will become more and more refined. It is not about crude matter, it is not about the crude material world; the more refined the material world that you enjoy, the more refined the happiness it gives. That is the lesson in detachment.

Q: Yes, I understand. For instance when one uses alcohol or drugs, the enjoyment they give is crude, and enjoying this kind of thing can be reduced more and more.

To return to what You said regarding my cat; I love that animal, so when she is gone, I am sad. I am not detached then, but still, love is something good, isn't it? I find that contradictory and then You say, "You have a right to be sad, that does not determine your attachment".

B: Yes, that is correct. The attachment is determined by the degree of confidence you may or may not have.

Q: The confidence that things will turn out all right?

B: Not necessarily.

Q: That it is good the way it is, even if it entails sadness?

B: Yes.

Q: Even that it is good to be sad?

B: Yes, even that. Detachment in this case is trusting that being sad about something essential, and an animal or a human being always is, that this sadness has been willed by God and therefore is good.

214

Q: Yes, now I am starting to get it. So, detachment is accepting everything that happens as it happens. Sadness and fear as well. Not thinking, "oh, I am sad" or "oh, I am anxious, therefore I am not detached", but rather, "oh, I am sad" or "oh, I am anxious, let me have confidence that God wants me to undergo this and that it is good for me".

B: Yes, that is the lesson.

Suddenly I find myself in the old dilemma again; is it Baba or am I the one who is answering the questions? Then I think "what does it matter, it gives me clarity and that's what it is all about".

Q: Maybe that is also detachment, not worrying whether it is Baba or not?

B: It certainly is, you surrender yourself then to BEING, to whom you are. Let that proceed. Go on with it, never stop. That is your path towards me, which I accompany at every moment; whether you are aware of it or not is not important.

Q: It is indeed very pleasant to correspond with You in this quiet and peaceful way, but if my cat would still be missing, I couldn't have done it.

B: No, and that is what you should have accepted then. Confidence is accepting that things are as they are, that you feel the way you feel. You don't need to be someone else, be yourself.

Q: And what if this "being yourself" is still riddled with faults and imperfections?

B: Happy is he who accepts himself with his faults and imperfections.

Q: But don't we have to fight these. Don't we have to become better human beings?

B: Fighting your faults and imperfections can only be done once you have accepted you have them.

Q: Yes, but that is not the same as accepting yourself *with* these faults and imperfections.

B: It is the same. By accepting yourself with your faults and imperfections, by feeling love for the Self, you will quite naturally want to work on those faults and that way they will disappear one by one.

Q: But what if you don't accept yourself but still wish to work on your faults? What about that?

B: If you don't accept yourself, if you don't love yourself *with* your faults, you will not be able to remove your faults. The faults will then take possession of you. It is not you anymore who accepts yourself, it is the faults that accept you. When you don't love yourself, you will only be able to repress your faults. However, that will cause them to return in all vehemence, which will result in you making even more faults and that way you will have ended up in a vicious circle.

Q: So, You say, "love yourself, even with the worst faults".

B: Yes, love yourself, don't love your faults, though. Accept your faults as belonging to you. You are who you are *with* those faults. That way you are going to experience the necessity of becoming a better person. You are going to want to remove those faults. Precisely because you love yourself.

Q: You talk about the lower, common self, I suppose, not the Higher?

B: Is there a difference?

Q: Yes, I think so.

B: That is the error of thought you make. Loving oneself is the same as loving one's Self.

Q: But the Higher Self (in capitals) doesn't have any faults, does it?

B: That now is exactly the method of becoming faultless. Love yourself with your faults and they will disappear as snow before the sun.

Q: But what about hard-core criminals then? They love themselves and their deeds, how can that be good?

B: They don't love themselves, that's why they commit these acts; that is the great problem and the tragedy of it. They were never taught to love themselves.

Q: But they love their deeds.

B: They don't love their deeds. Through their deeds they externalize the discontent that rages in them.

Q: So, You say that they should love themselves *with* those terrible deeds they commit or have committed?

B: Yes that is the way to transcend those deeds.

Q: Is there someone who can teach them how?

B: God can teach them.

Q: So, they should turn to God then?

B: That's evident, isn't it?

Q: Yes, that is true. But then how is it when we look at it from a Karmic point of view? Shouldn't they atone for their deeds?

B: When atonement is accepted as coming from God, as the grace of God, even the worst inconvenience, the worst pain, is bearable.

Q: So, here also it comes down to being confident that whatever happens is good the way it happens.

B: Yes.

Q: Quite difficult, Baba, for I think that You also say then that it is good that there are victims who must undergo those terrible things, that perhaps it is to be imputed to their Karma and I find it very hard to put it that way.

B: No, that is not how it is. Every person who has complete confidence in God will be helped by Him, even in the most critical circumstance; things will be made light for him. How and why something happens need not be clear in all cases, isn't clear most of the time, especially not to outsiders. Somebody else may and can never judge which Karma is reserved for whom. A terrible event does not automatically mean that this is to be imputed to this person's bad Karmic development. The outsider does not know anything about it and should not pass judgement if he doesn't want to be judged himself by his own measure. Leave to God why things happen, only trust that it is good as it is, no matter how terrible what may befall someone else.

Q: And what about innocent children?

B: No one is without guilt and no one is with guilt; guilt does not exist. There is an everlasting existence which suffers a burden or which imposes a burden on someone else. Being focused on God reduces the burden, whether it is to be suffered or whether you are the one who imposes it on someone else. The outcome is always up to God, who makes all things - let that be clear, all things - light for the person who is focused on Him.

Q: And that is the person who accepts himself and all his faults?

B: Yes, that is the person who knows that he comes from God, that God loves him with his faults and that through God's love his faults will disappear, one by one.

I have been thinking about this for a while and then an inner dialogue starts up again.

217

Q: Baba, I love life. I don't want to detach myself from it at all and what You just said is that I don't need to do so. It is wonderful to be living. With every fibre of my being I love life, existence, BEING, nature.

B: Good, that is the beginning of detachment.

Q: How is that?

B: You are on your way of detaching yourself from wanting to be detached. You are accepting what and who you are with your attachments. You no longer want something you are not.

Q: And that is being detached?

B: Yes, being detached means accepting who you are.

Q: Well, in my case that is easy, my greatest problem seems to be that my cat was gone for a couple of days. But what about others, who really have bad things happening to them?

B: You also have had really bad things happen to you in your life.

Q: Yes, that is true, but at that time I wasn't able to accept them.

B: Yes you were, you accepted God in that period.

Q: Yes, that's correct, but I was convinced that He had forsaken me.

B: You recognized His existence, though.

Q: Yes, that's true.

B: Which means that you accept Him in your existence, whether you want to acknowledge it as such or not. How can you recognize God's existence and at the same time exist without Him? That is impossible. When you recognize God's existence, He exists through your existence. Should you not exist, you wouldn't be able to recognize God. So, it is thanks to you that God exists.

Q: And this can be said by everyone who recognizes God's existence?

B: Yes, of course.

Q: But if I didn't exist, God could still exist, couldn't He?

B: You wouldn't be able to recognize this fact, though. That's what it is about. The individual recognition that God exists, is what makes Him exist. In every life anew.

Q: That seems distorted logic to me.

B: No, it is quite essential. That's what makes it so important that man recognizes God. When God is not recognized, God keeps aloof from that person. Because when man denies God's existence, God does indeed not exist.

Q: But didn't You also create those people and isn't it true that someone can change?

B: Yes, at all times God's existence in man can be recognized. And yes, I created everything and everyone; with free will however. Free will to recognize God's existence yes or no.

Q: Is that the ultimate free will?

B: Yes, that's what everything boils down to eventually.

Q: But when someone is good, only does good deeds, but doesn't recognize God's existence, then that isn't really wrong, is it?

B: When someone is good and does good in that manner, he accepts God. He accepts what's good and good is a form of God.

Q: Yes, yes, it does not matter which form of God you worship, recognize, as long as it is a God-form.

B: Precisely.

Q: Let me recapitulate, enjoying life is allowed; enjoying life is a form of detachment. Detachment from wanting to be detached?

B: Enjoying life means living each moment to the full, being detached from past and future. Enjoying life is a state of BEING.

Q: With enjoying life I mean indeed enjoying BEING itself, not enjoying the things that facilitate or seem to facilitate life and I take it that everything was meant in that context?

B: Yes.

Q: Yes, for otherwise one would not say "I love life" but, "I love my car, my music, my house" and so on. So, that's the difference?

B: That's right.

Q: So, loving life is the state of BEING to which You so often refer?

B: Yes.

Q: And this is so because then one lives in the present?

B: Precisely.

Q: But that isn't always possible.

B: Try to experience it as often as possible; should this not be the case, be confident that is good as well. Do not worry about other states of BEING. Be who you are at any moment.

Q: But I must keep observing myself?

B: Of course.

Q: But surely when I am in such a state of BEING, I'm not observing myself?

B: Why not?

Q: Then I AM.

B: Then you know that you ARE, which means you are observing yourself.

Q: Knowledge is observance?

B: That's a way to express it, yes.

59
EVERYTHING IS EXISTING AT ONCE

3 October 1996

I was thinking about the state of BEING and I have come to the following conclusion: everything is One, BEING is One and everlasting. That is what Baba says. But we don't experience it as such because in our existence BEING is constantly broken down into fragments. Whereas at the same time it is One. Everything we experience, see, hear, feel, including getting older and dying, forms part of BEING, which is One. Everything is as it is and not something else. Nothing can be changed, even though everything changes continuously. I think that that is what Baba means when He says, "No blade of grass can be picked without me willing it".

Question: Is that true, Baba?

Baba: Yes.

Q: You want me to write about this?

B: No, not yet, let it sink in. It is too difficult to describe in words. It doesn't belong to the intellect but to BEING.

How then do you want to express it in words? It forms part of BEING.

Q: You mean: it has been thought up by me now - in as far as I am capable of it - and now it forms part of unity, the way everything does.

B: Yes.

Q: It seems as if I get it and don't get it at the same time. As if I am about to grasp it any minute and then I actually grasp nothing.

B: That is exactly what happens.

Q: But if all I can do is experience it, it cannot be explained to others.

B: That is correct. It is a fact of experience.

Q: Will people recognize in each other that they have experienced it?

B: No, that is not necessary, there are as many states of experiencing it as there are people.

Q: So, one experiences BEING individually and the world just keeps on going as it always has?

B: That's right.

Q: But when everybody, every person on earth, is experiencing BEING, then what?

B: Even when that would would happen, the world would still keep on going. Compare it to a film that is projected on a screen. The film already exists, has been waiting in a tin all this time, is projected on a screen and stored away again.

Q: So, all of life with its billions and billions of years past and years to come already exists?

B: Yes.

Q: The film is stored in a tin, takes up hardly any room and even less time and when one wants to watch it, it takes two hours and a screen is needed; is that comparable to space and time?

B: Yes.

Q: How then, Baba?

B: Space is like the projection-screen, time - those billions and billions of years - is similar to the time it takes to project the film.

Q: But who is the spectator, for whom has the film been made?

B: God is the spectator. God divided Himself into 1. man, creative man, who is also permitted to be a spectator, but who is in the first instance an actor in the creation, as it were, and 2. into divine consciousness, which remains a spectator and which directs the whole.

Q: But surely God can intervene in individual lives?

B: That forms part of unity. That had already been stored in the film.

Q: Does that imply then that nothing can change, that everything is totally preordained?

B: No, the film is made and projected at the same time. That's the difference. That's where the analogy ends.

Q: So, I should imagine that we are watching a film that is made at the same moment?

B: Yes.

Q: And once it has been made, it belongs to the ineffacable data of that film?

B: Yes.

Q: And so everything is changeable and one whole at the same time, seen in retrospect that is?

B: Yes. However, since in essence time doesn't exist, there is no "retrospect" and everything exists at once.

Q: I could understand it by putting it this way: despite the fact that the reel of film can be constantly changed, it is also already completely in existence.

B: Yes, that comes close to what can be said about it in words.

Q: And, once we know that we are God, we can also enjoy the film as spectators, even though we are creating the film ourselves continuously, whereas when we don't know yet that we are God, everything that happens to us seems to befall us, is that how it is?

B: Yes.

Q: But who has thought that up and why?

B: Things were never thought up, there is one everlasting state of BEING in which time and space fall away and everything is compressed, just picture it like that.

Q: So, BEING is even more compressed than the reel on which the film is stored?

B: Infinitely more compressed. That reel of film takes up space; what takes up space, takes up time as well.

Q: I don't understand that, Baba, can You explain that further?

B: Time is bound up with space, everything that takes up space influences time. Just as everything that takes up time influences space.

Q: Even when it is about something very small?

223

B: Yes, even then.

Q: So, creating things is what requires time and space?

B: Yes and no.

Q: What do You mean?

-No answer

Q: Baba, won't You answer this?

B: This can't be answered, because it is fundamentally different. It is true, because it is said and understood as such. Hence the answer "yes". Creation, however, is in itself not subject to time and space, transcends time and space, is that what is being seen—in your eyes in retrospect—and what has always existed. In that respect the answer is "no".

Q: So, the riddle is never solved?

B: No, not with the intellect. Give it up, this "wanting to know". Experience it and realise how simple and easy it is as long as you don't need to understand.

60
SPEAK AS LITTLE AS POSSIBLE

25 October 1996

Lately I have been confronted with the fact that different people often tell me contradictory things, while they all think of themselves as being right. I can't really manage to have any understanding of this, let alone love. Love for people rather happens to me when I am looking at people, whether I know them or not; then sometimes this overwhelming feeling of love wells up. This brings me to the conclusion that in order to develop love for one's fellow human beings - and isn't that what Baba wants from us all? - it is better that this takes place non-verbally.

Question: Is this true, Baba?

Baba: Yes.

Q: Does this hold good for everyone?

B: For everyone, always; words distract.

Q: So, it is better not to speak.

B: Speak only when it is necessary, keep quiet otherwise. Use your energy sparingly when it comes to speaking.

Q: And listening?

B: Listen without passing judgement, without judging who is right or wrong at whatever time; that is totally unimportant. For love to flow paying attention to the soul is required, not to what presents itself in the world of phenomena.

61
FORBEARANCE

16 December 1996

I just had a confrontation with X, who was extremely unreasonable. I could not help getting angry. After X left, a feeling of tiredness and powerlessness came over me. I realized I would have done better not to become angry, that anger is an emotion which is most exhausting. I decided to place what just happened before Baba. He explains how I could have handled the situation better.

Question: When I correspond with You in this way, the anger and this feeling of powerlessness flow away from me.

Baba: That was the intention.

Q: I realize now that it was the unreasonableness that angered me most. Maybe the lesson is that I am now learning that I am no match against unreasonableness, especially not when it is accompanied by conceitedness and that I had better let things rest then.

B: Yes, that is the lesson.

Q: Could it be that there is unreasonableness in me then, that that's what makes me react so vehemently?

B: No, there isn't any. Look at Jesus, wasn't it the greatest unreasonableness of all to nail Him to the cross? Now that doesn't imply that Jesus was unreasonable, does it?

Q: But I can hardly compare myself to Jesus, can I?

B: Why not? For that purpose He sacrificed himself, that people would find support in His suffering and would uplift themselves because of it.

Q: Yes, He really was the lamb that was led to the slaughter, and that's how - on a small scale - I also feel now. And then the haughtiness with which X justified his wrong working method! In those times it must also have been like that. Of course those Pharisees also thought that they were utterly right. How is it possible!

B: That is the nature of man. Be like Jesus, endure it kindly.

Q: When You are with me as You are now (while writing my heart has started to glow), I am capable of it, but just now when X was here, I did not feel You with me.

B: I wanted you to go through the experience. I also wanted you to go through the experience that anger against this kind of person is of no avail. That it only reverberates upon yourself.

Q: You say, "against this kind of person". Does that mean that sometimes anger does serve a purpose?

B: Certainly, sometimes anger is justified. However, on the condition that the other person grasps what it is all about. Someone like X has not reached that stage yet. Let that be enough. Never enter into a discussion with X again. You will get the worst of it and become exhausted, even though you are right.

Q: Baba, You are a great comfort. Please help me lose my ego. Teach me to be as "meek" as Jesus. As forbearing and loving.

B: The lesson is not going *against* but going *with*, going with the stream, not swimming against it.

Q: Does that mean going with the unreasonableness?

B: Yes, that's the way to expose it.

Q: Should I become unreasonable myself then?

B: No, you go along with it by repeating it. That way someone may - perhaps realize his error. If that should not be so, you withdraw.

Q: How do You mean that?

B: You withdraw from the argument, leave it to others.

Q: Should I express this in words?

B: No, do it, don't talk about it.

Q: Baba, I want to progress further towards You. How do I go about it? How in devotion grow?

B: Dedicate everything to me, trust my omniscience.

Q: You also know what just happenend?

B: Of course I know. I am in everything and everyone.

Q: But if You are also in X, why then is he so unreasonable?

B: That is the nature of Maya. Man's nature is tied up with the world of phenomena. This nature can only be redirected through the course of many lives. First insight into one's own failings will have to be developed. When Maya-nature predominates, God withdraws. God sees, but allows man the freedom to develop insight into his faults himself, only then can improvement occur.

Q: And that may take many lives?

B: Bad qualities can be very persistent. And by being confronted again and again by what one is doing wrong, man will eventually realize that he is on the wrong track.

Q: But shouldn't someone else confront that person then with the wrong he is doing?

B: That someone else has to wage his own war against his own nature. For one person confrontation will be the way. For another person the way is "being non-confrontive". Try to find out within yourself how your devotion can grow. It is never so that one single person can make another person realize his faults. Many situations in many lives see to that. Man who thinks that he can make another person realize something is on the wrong track. Do not lend yourself to this. When a situation threatens to get out of hand because of a wrong deed of another person, you may intervene to save the situation, not that other person. Situations are the learning-processes in which the interaction of people with one another is required. The interest of the whole is what is at stake.

Q: But what if one makes mistakes in doing so?

B: Direct the process in a friendly manner, but never be so sure of yourself that you think you can make another person change his nature. Situations are for that, many situations in many lives. Try to redirect situations, never the people in them.

Q: But it is the people who create such situations, isn't it? Don't we have to go against such people then?

B: As said before, by going with the stream, by allowing the situation to exist for some time, it will wear out by itself.

Q: But isn't that precisely why wars originate and continue to exist?

B: Exactly.

228

Q: But isn't that terrible?

B: That is the way it is and no other way. Who should be judged responsible and by whom to prevent a war? Man who is at the root of the breaking out of such war, will have to develop this insight himself.

Q: But that could happen at the expense of many, many lives.

B: Each life in each situation has also to learn its own lesson from such a situation. It can never be that any given situation only originated because one person made a mistake. Everyone can learn his own lesson from each process, from each situation.

Q: I find that hard to understand. We see things happen because of the fact that someone is doing something wrong. We should not turn against that one person then, but we should intervene in the process if the situation threatens to get out of hand. And when we are not able to do so, we should let the situation continue and we should realize that that also has a function in which everyone can learn his lesson. But how does one let such a situation continue?

B: By not going against it if it is to no avail. No good is to be derived from such act. Only God can influence man. Man may think that he does so, but it is God who moves everything and everyone.

62
UNITY

14 March 1997

I know that I am going towards becoming one with God. I experience that unity more and more. But what I don't experience, though, is its attendant awareness of being one with all beings. Sitting in front of my altar I think about this and meditate on it. "How is that, Baba, does that mean that I am not yet on the path of becoming one with You then?" At that moment I suddenly see in my meditation a large heart (the muscle-shape, not the heart-shape) and I understand that God, the Father, and I are one in my heart. That that is this lovely, all-overwhelming feeling of bliss in my heart. "And," it goes on in my thoughts, "if He and I are one in my heart and He is in everyone's heart, then I am in everyone's heart. That is unity. I am not all the other people, but I am in the heart of everything else. There is only one heart."

Question: It remains difficult, when I think about this, Baba; will You clear it up for me?

Baba: Yes.

Q: How is that? Please explain it to me.

B: The heart is the place where love assembles, where it concentrates, where it merges in God.

Q: But what does that have to do with other people?

B: Everything and nothing. For there are no other people, there is only love

Q: Yes, but how can I experience unity with all, with all beings?

B: By concentrating on the unity in your own heart. It is about spiritual unity That must be experienced.

Q: And what if people do odd things, play strange tricks with which I totally disagree, and I don't feel that unity, what then? Is it actually important to fee that unity?

B: No, important is to BE that unity.

Q: Is that how we can reach spiritual unity with all beings? By BEING unity?

B: Yes, by uniting with God in your heart. By feeling one with God.

Q: So, I only need to concentrate on my own heart; on this soft, sweet, burning feeling in my heart. That is sufficient to experience spiritual unity with all beings?

B: Yes, that is enough. Keep concentrating on me in your heart. Keep focused on your heart, on me in your heart, in all your decisions. Know that you and I are one. Do not go by what others do or say. Consult in everything your own heart. That is the way to unity. The fastest way to God. Everything in life comes down to that. That is the great aim of life.

EPILOGUE

Baba and God... When He is with me in my heart, it is formless and it is God. Baba says that He is God. He has brought me to God. He is the Sadguru; so, He is God. There is no contradiction whatsoever. Still, lately I have often named what I experience God. Whoever Baba is - and why couldn't God, who is almighty, manifest himself on earth in a human body? - He is for sure the Sadguru who brings people back to a living God-realisation. Who teaches people the divine values and makes them apply them. So, He is God. It cannot be otherwise.

Baba is in my heart as God. All the time. There are no questions anymore at the moment. So, no lessons anymore either. That is good. For me it really means a step forward. I am on the way of becoming one with Him. I am in blissful expectation of Him. "Your Ananda is my Ananda," Baba often says. So, He too enjoys this, knows this. It is really love which flows over from one to the other. He is me, I am Him. The Ananda is mutual. There is one heart in which we love each other - God and I. It is almost too good to be true. But it is true. And for this purpose we have all been created! Maybe you, who read those words, also experience it and maybe the recognition of it gives you great joy and the certainty that you walk the right path. Time falls away. We have been living in the house of our Father, God, through the ages. The walls of time have fallen away. There is really one everlasting state of BEING, to which we may bear witness.

It is not important that my name is Geesje Lunshof. What difference does it make what name I have! Any name would do. It is important that I share the God-experience with you. That I may write about how God is a reality in our heart. How we are one with Him. It really exists and it is the most beautiful, purest, sweetest thing that could happen to someone. Doubt is no longer possible. For this we were created. And all the pain and sorrow we have had to cope with was worth the suffering. Thank You God, thank You, thank You, thank You.

The Hague
April 1997

233

GLOSSARY

Ananda	Joy, divine bliss.
Anandamayakosa	The fifth kosa (inner layer) of the body, which consists of bliss.
Anima	The unconscious female part in a human being (Jung).
Animus	The unconscious male part in a human being (Jung).
A-dharmic	That which goes against the law of Dharma.
Ashram	A religious community, where people gather around a Guru.
Atma	The Self, the soul, the spark of God within. The reality behind appearances, universal and immanent in every being.
Avatar	God taking birth in human form. Sai Baba is considered an Avatar.
Bhagavad Gita	The Hindu "Gospel". The Song of God. It is a small chapter in the Indian epic Mahabharata, where Lord Krishna explains to Arjuna the eternal teachings of God.
Bhajans	Devotional songs in praise of God.
Bhajan-service	A religious ceremony, during which bhajans are sung. Usually one singer sings a line, which is then sung in chorus by those present.
Bhakta	A devotee who has fully surrendered to God.
Bhakti	Devotion.
Bhakti-yoga	The yoga or discipline of devotion. An attitude to life of complete surrender; everything one does is dedicated to God.
Buddhi	The discriminating faculty of the mind.
Chakra	Circle, wheel. Center of potential energy in the human body. The seven main chakras are situated from the base of the spine to the crown of the head.
Darshan	To see a holy person and receive his blessing.
Dharma	Righteousness, the moral code of conduct according to which man should live, which ensures inner purification and harmony. When truth (Sathya) is put into practice, it is called Dharma.
Dharmic	Living in accordance with the law of Dharma.
Dhyana Vahini	A book on meditation written by Sai Baba.
Gopis	The cowmaids or milkmaids who were companions

	and ardent devotees of Krishna.
Gunas	Qualities or characteristics. There are three Gunas: Satwa (harmony), Rajas (activity) and Tamas (passiveness), to which everything that lives is subject.
Jivatma	The soul in the individual.
Jnana	Wisdom, spiritual knowledge.
Jnana-yoga	The yoga or discipline of knowledge about the Self, which leads to knowledge about uniting with God.
Kali Yuga	The present age, known as the age of iron or darkness. The age in which the earth has reached its lowest point, when Dharma is totally ignored. In the Bhagavad Gita (the age-old holy book of the Hindus) it is mentioned that, when the earth has reached this stage, the Avatar Krishna will come again. This has now happened with the coming of Sathya Sai Baba.
Karma	The law of cause and effect of all our deeds, actions and thoughts. Whatever you sow you will reap in this or a next life, both good and bad.
Karma-yoga	The yoga or discipline of action. An attitude to life in which everything one does is carried out without attaching importance to the result.
Kosa	A sheath, a cover. There are five kosas which, together with the ensheathed Atma, constitute the body.
Kurukshetra	The battlefield in the Mahabharata (the famous Hindu-epic), where the great battle between the Pandavas and the Kauravas was fought. Symbolically it is the battlefield of contradictory forces in man; here the lower nature, the ego, must be purified.
Mantra	A sacred word or collection of sacred words, which can be meditated upon through continual repetition. Any one of the countless names of God can serve the purpose.
Maya	Illusion. The world of appearances in which nothing is permanent. The transient which is mistaken for the eternal.
Paramatma	The universal soul. God. The Absolute from which everything has emanated, in which all exists and into which all will merge again.
Prakriti	The Cosmic Substance. Creation. The objective world. Nature.
Prana	The vital air which we inhale. The breath of God.
Prashanti Nilayam	The name of Sai Baba's ashram, next to the village of Puttaparthi. The name means: abode of supreme peace.

Prema Sai	The next incarnation of Sathya Sai Baba. As predicted, His is a triple incarnation. Sai Baba first came as Shirdi Sai Baba. He lived in that form from 838 until 1918. Now He is on earth as Sathya Sai Baba. He has said that He will live to be 95. He then will return as Prema Sai Baba.
Puttaparthi	A village in South India where Sai Baba was born and where His ashram is situated.
Puja	Worshipping God according to certain rituals, such as the offering of flowers and/or food.
Purusha	The Supreme. The Creator of the universe. The eternal Conscious Principle.
Rajas	Action, energy, commotion; one of the three gunas.
Ramakrishna	A great Indian saint, who lived from 1836 till 1886.
Sadguru	The true teacher who leads the seeker towards liberation.
Sadhaka	A spiritual aspirant. One who is practising the discipline of conquering his sense of "I" or "mine".
Sadhana	Spiritual discipline.
Sadhu	A saintly person; generally used to indicate a monk.
Sankalpa	Divine will. God's wish, grace.
Satwa	Purity, harmony, blissfulness, the essence of BEING; one of the three gunas.
Seva	Voluntary, selfless service. Baba says, "Hands that help are holier than lips that pray".
Shakti	The power or energy-aspect of God.
Shiva	God. The destroying and renovating aspect of Brahman, the Hindu Trinity, the other two being Brahma, the creating aspect, and Vishnu the preserving aspect. Sai Baba is both Avatar of Vishnu and of Shiva. There is no difference in fact. God (Brahman) is One without a second.
Swami	Master.
Tamas	Passiveness, inertia, dullness; one of the three gunas.
Vibuthi	The sacred ash which Baba materialises for his devotees and which has curative power. Ash is symbolic for detachment. It is the ultimate reality after matter has been burned. Likewise we should reduce all our desires to ash in order to live in a pure and divine manner.
Whitefield	A village in India near Bangalore where Sai Baba has a second Ashram.
Yogi	A spiritual aspirant who is God-centered and seeks union with God by means of one or more forms of yoga.

INDEX
(numbered per chapter)

Sai-consciousness 54,55,57
saints 21
scientists 42
the Second Coming 20
seeing oneself in others 24
the Self 19,26,27,28,42,54
self-confidence 42
self-knowledge 43
self-realisation 42
self-sacrifice 42
self-satisfaction 42
separation 40,54,59
Seva 14
Shakti 14,40
Shiva 12,14,40
situations 61
to speak 60
speaking through someone 22,24
being a spectator 44,45,59
the speed of light 44
Spirit 28
spiritual pride 51
stars 54
the state of BEING 13,14,19,29,
    35,46,53,56,57,58,59
the story of Christ 11
sub-atoms 19
subjectivity 21
to suffer 8,20,28.32.45,48,50,58
surrender 11,19
the swing 12
symbols 1.19
to take action 22
THAT 19,21
to think 39
not thinking 44

thoughts 44
time/space 8,28,33,39,54,59
timeless 54
being tired 29
the totality 50
toxins
transformation 12,29,54
transparent 53,54
to trust 13,14,23,49,55,56,58
truth 19,22,54
the TV-news 45
TV-programme 49
unity/oneness 8,10,19,29,40,
    57,59,69
the universe 50,54
unreasonableness 61
vibration 28
vibration level 40
victims 61
victory 26
visions 22
waking consciousness 19
to want to know 59
war 16,33,48,61
wavering 27
why 19,29,55,56
why God comes to earth 24
why go to Baba 54
will-less 50
words 40,59
to work in public 42
the world 46,59
wrong interpretation 63
youth 10